The Macroeconomy: A Business Perspective

The Macroeconomy: A Business Perspective
3rd Edition

Keith Cuthbertson
Newcastle University
Peter Gripaios
Plymouth Business School

INTERNATIONAL THOMSON BUSINESS PRESS
I ⓣ P®An International Thomson Publishing Company

London • Bonn • Boston • Johannesburg • Madrid • Melbourne • Mexico City • New York • Paris
Singapore • Tokyo • Toronto • Albany, NY • Belmont, CA • Cincinnati, OH • Detroit, MI

The Macroeconomy: A Business Perspective
Copyright © 1997 Keith Cuthbertson and Peter Gripaios

First published by International Thomson Business Press

Business Press is a division of Thomson Learning.
The Thomson Learning logo is a registered trademark used herein under licence.

British Library Cataloguing in Publication Data
A catalogue record for this book is available from the British Library

First edition 1997

Typeset by J&L Composition Ltd, Filey, North Yorkshire
Printed in Croatia by Zrinski d.d., Čakovec

ISBN 186-152-0883

Thomson Learning
Berkshire House
168-173 High Holborn
London WC1V 7AA
UK

http://www.thomsonlearning.com

Contents

Figures

Tables

Abbreviations

AD	aggregate demand
AS	aggregate supply
CAPM	capital asset pricing policy
CBI	Confederation of British Industry
CIP	covered interest rate parity
DAD	dynamic aggregate demand
DLAS	long-run dynamic aggregate supply
DSAS	short-run dynamic aggregate supply
ERM	exchange rate mechanism
EU	European Union
FOREX	foreign exchange
FRA	forward rate agreement
GATT	General Agreement on Tariffs and Trade
GDP	gross domestic product
HPY	holding period yield
IMF	International Monetary Fund
IRR	internal rate of return
LAS	long-run aggregate supply
NAIRU	non-accelerating inflation rate of unemployment
NIESR	National Institute of Economic and Social Research
NPV	net present value
OECD	Organization for Economic Co-operation and Development
OPEC	Organization of Petroleum Exporting Countries
PPP	purchasing power parity
PSBR	public sector borrowing requirement
RE	rational expectations
RPI	retail price index
SAS	short-run aggregate supply
UIP	uncovered interest rate parity
VAR	vector autoregressive
VAT	value added tax

Introduction

1

There are, of course, numerous economics texts designed for the economics specialist but until very recently few had been designed specifically for business persons or students in the business area. And yet economics has very often been an important component of degrees in subjects such as business studies, accountancy and marketing, and of professional courses. It may be argued that there is a huge gap between the economics taught on a specialist economics degree course and the economic concepts that are used by business persons and, even, business economists. Frequently, the complaint of business-orientated students is the lack of relevance of much of the economics taught on conventional courses, a complaint which deserves much sympathy. However, economic matters and the macroeconomic environment in particular are of considerable importance to the practising businessman. The challenge is, therefore, to design useful courses in economics for business, bearing in mind both the non-specialist audience and the typically limited time available in which to get the message across. This task is attempted here. The book is developed as follows. First, some theoretical foundations are laid down which will be useful for understanding economic issues and the more applied chapters which constitute the rest of the book. The latter begin with an examination of macroeconomic risk including the business cycle and its effects on business. It is suggested that the macroeconomic environment is of great importance to business profitability and it is, therefore, crucial that the business person understands that environment.

Forward planning is of some importance to business and this brings us on to the potential role of forecasting. We, therefore, examine macroeconomic forecasts and their usefulness in business decision-taking, including their use in scenario-planning and sensitivity analysis. We then turn to a detailed examination of the international environment with a chapter on the exchange rate. This examines the impact of exchange rates on business and exchange rate, economic fundamentals before turning to a look at economic forecasting models and, finally, to risk avoidance strategies.

The next chapter follows this pattern and deals with the financial environment. It examines in turn the impact of changing interest rates on firms, interest rate fundamentals, forecasts and, again, risk avoidance. There is particular consideration of new approaches to explaining the behaviour of financial markets.

Policy considerations are given detailed consideration after this. First we consider controversies regarding the role of economic policy in economic growth, which is of clear importance to business people. We also examines types of policy and particular policy issues including the case for a European single currency and for regional policy. The overview then brings together the points made in previous chapters in the context of improving knowledge and control of the business environment.

Where possible the intention has been to make the book free standing although readers would certainly benefit from having studied an introductory book on economics and perhaps also one on introductory statistics.

The new edition differs in a number of respects from the last. Many chapters have been extensively rewritten and there is now explicit consideration of the importance of chaos theory. We have again included self-assessment questions, some of which require an extension of the material outlined in the text. These can be used in conjunction with the further reading referred to as well as other sources such as recent journal and newspaper articles. The new edition contains some boxed sections giving more information on some issues referred to in the main text.

We hope that the book will at the very least enable business persons and business students to understand economic articles in the press. They may even be able to satisfactorily answer the questions of the man or woman in the pub, something far too many economics graduates are unable to do.

Economic foundations $\boxed{2}$

The ideas of economists and political philosophers, both when they are right and when they are wrong, are more powerful than is commonly understood. Indeed the world is ruled by little else. Practical men, who believe themselves to be quite exempt from any intellectual influences, are usually the slave of some defunct economist. Madmen in authority, who hear voices in the air, are distilling their frenzy from some academic scribbler of a few years back.

(John Maynard Keynes)

Many people think of economics as an exact science and find it extremely irritating that one group of economists disagrees with another group and that economists and, therefore, the Governments they advise so often get things wrong. The fact, however, is that the nature of economic relationships is extremely complex and, therefore, difficult to fathom. Moreover, what may be true at one period of time is not necessarily true at others, for behaviour is sometimes altered quite dramatically in response to changes in fashion, tastes and other economic shocks.

This all gives plenty of scope for individual economists to hold different theoretical perceptions regarding which economic variables are most important, which economic variable is affected by which other economic variable(s) and to what extent and for what reason at a particular time. It has also made such perceptions difficult to refute by statistical testing despite early optimism that such refutation would be possible. In short, economics, despite a sizeable scientific component, remains very much an art and we should not expect it to be otherwise.

Nevertheless, the effects of the art are obvious in the form of economic forecasts and economic policies, and the latter, in particular, can affect the livelihood of millions. It is of some importance, therefore, that time is spent looking at the important schools of economic thought. To do this we develop, in simple terms, four economic models.

Any macroeconomic model is a simple representation of very complex and ineffectively understood real world economic processes so that assumptions and definitions made at the outset determine the conclusion of any one model. We now examine the four selected models in turn, three in the main text and one in the appendix at the end of this chapter.

2.1 THE CLASSICAL MODEL

This model is based on the Quantity Theory of money which can be traced back to the writings of David Hume (1711–76). It is based on the so-called Fisher equation:

$$MV = PT \qquad (2.1)$$

where M = quantity of money in circulation
V = velocity of circulation of money
P = the average price level (rate per transaction)
T = the number of transactions per period

This has to be true by definition (i.e. it really is an identity) and is easily explained as follows. Suppose that 100 million transactions take place in the course of a year at an average price of £4. In this case P × T = £400 million which is the value of goods sold during the year. If the total quantity of money in circulation is just £100 million, then each unit of money must on average be circulating 400/100 = 4 times per annum.

Box 2.1 Definitions of money

These have often been changed in an era when inflation and its causes has focused attention on the various monetary aggregates. One cause has been rapid and significant changes in asset-holding behaviour as markets have become deregulated. A second is a wish of governments to define something they could, for a while, seem to target as a control variable. In the UK, the following definitions currently apply:

MO   Notes and coins in circulation
       Bankers deposits with the Bank of England for operational
       purposes
NIBMI Non-bank private sector holdings of notes and coins
       Non-interest bearing 'sight' deposits held by UK depositors
       with UK banks
M2   Non-bank, non-building society, private sector holdings of
       notes and coins
       UK private sector retail deposits held with UK banks and
       building societies
M4   Notes and coins in circulation
       All non-bank, non-building society private sector sterling
       deposits (= retail and wholesale)
M3M   M4 plus private sector foreign currency bank and building
       society deposits plus all sterling and foreign currency deposits
       held by UK public corporations with UK banks and building
       societies
M5   M4 plus private sector holdings of bank bills, Treasury bills,
       local authority deposits, national savings and certificates of tax
       deposit

Equation (2.1) must *always* hold, because we have defined V as PT/M. MV = PT is in fact an **identity**, in the sense that MV and PT must always be the same as one another, regardless of what is happening in the economy.

The classical theorists argued that T and V in the long-run would be independent of what happens to M. They argued that other factors such as improvements in productivity and the introduction of new products would be necessary to increase T and that increases in M would merely affect the price level P.

More modern versions of the Quantity Theory respecify (2.1) as:

$$M = KPY \tag{2.2}$$

Thus K = 1/V and Y = real income (or output) is substituted for the number of transactions.

It should be noted that, in multiplicative functions of this type, the proportional rate of change in the left-hand side variable is the sum of the proportional rates of change in the non-constant terms on the right-hand side. Thus:

$$m = p + y \tag{2.3}$$

where *m*, *p* and *y* are defined as the per cent changes in respective variables.

Therefore if, as the classical economists suggest, Y is relatively fixed, then an increase in the money supply of 12 per cent will lead to price inflation of 12 per cent.

However, the main justification for the classical view was that economies should always be operating at full capacity level. If this was not so it was because factors such as labour were demanding too high a real wage, meaning that some workers were priced out of the market and unemployed. As long as the price of labour fell, it would be profitable to hire more labour and to sell the extra output produced by the extra workers.

This is, of course, simplistic and at odds with observation of the real world. For now it should be emphasized that (2.3) can result in a 12 per cent increase in the money supply being consistent with a 4 per cent increase in prices and an 8 per cent increase in output. This, of course, is more likely to be true in depressions when there is plenty of excess capacity around. Causation is an

---

Box 2.2 A stable velocity of circulation?

The classical economists always recognized that the velocity of circulation would fluctuate in the <u>short run</u>, particularly in response to sudden changes in the money stock. They and their monetarist successors have assumed it to be stable in the <u>long run</u>. Recent evidence suggests that this is arguable. The velocity of broad money aggregates such as M4 had been rising from the 1950s to the 1980s but has fallen dramatically in the 1980s and 1990s. One explanation is probably that, since 1980, short-term real interest rates have been high relative to previous periods thereby encouraging people to hold their wealth in interest-bearing deposits as opposed to non-monetary forms.

issue here. Critics would argue that causation could run from an increase in prices to an increase in the money supply rather than the other way around.

An added complication for the classical economists is that empirical studies suggest that V or, alternatively, K are not constant so that even if output was constant there would be no reason to expect increases in the money supply to cause one for one changes in prices. It is time to move on to a different approach.

Questions

1. Can the income of an economy be greater than the amount of money circulating in the system?
2. 'Given that the velocity of circulation is unstable, the quantity theory is not very useful.' Discuss.
3. Assume that the velocity of circulation is constant. If the money supply rises by 10 per cent in a year and there is a 4 per cent rise in output, by how much will inflation rise in the same year.

2.2   THE SIMPLE KEYNESIAN MODEL

This is the standard elementary textbook model with which some readers will no doubt be familiar. Though it is a gross oversimplification of 'Keynesian' economics and a parody of what Keynes actually wrote, it does bring out

---

Box 2.3 John Maynard Keynes (1883–1946)

John Maynard Keynes is perhaps the best known of all British economists. His great book the *General Theory of Employment, Interest and Money* (Keynes, 1936) was the foundation for the study of macroeconomics and is widely credited with having saved the capitalist system. The General Theory showed that, contrary to classical beliefs, an economy had no natural tendency to full employment and that there was a role for governments to intervene to create it.

This was not the first time Keynes had put forward controversial ideas. After the First World War he had been highly critical of German 'reparations' and subsequently he was critical of the decision by Winston Churchill to put Britain back on the Gold Standard at the pre-war rate of exchange. During the 1920s he lost and made and lost small fortunes on currency and stock speculation, and in the 1930s made huge gains on the Stock Exchange in the recovery from depression. Keynes also made large sums of money for his college, Kings, at Cambridge, again mainly in the 1930s.

Keynesian ideas were soon put into practice with the 'New Deal' in America, which was widely credited with ending the Great Depression there. In the UK and other parts of Europe increased public spending associated with rearmament had the same effect.

some of the essential points of the 'General Theory'. The model is based on an equilibrium between expenditure and income with all variables measured in real as opposed to monetary or nominal terms. For simplicity we assume for now, therefore, that prices are fixed. The equation for equilibrium is:

$$Y = C + I + G + X - M \qquad (2.4)$$

where Y = income

C = consumption

I = investment

G = government expenditure

X = exports

M = imports

Quite simply (2.4) states that, in equilibrium, income must equal expenditure on the grounds that what one man spends another receives as income. Should expenditure be less than income this time around then next period's income will be lower, and vice versa.

For simplicity, investment, government expenditure and exports can be regarded as exogenous but consumption is considered to be a function of disposable income (i.e. income after tax, T) and imports as a function of income in general. Thus the behavioural equations of the model are:

$$C = a + b [Y - T] \qquad (2.5)$$
$$I = I_0 \qquad (2.6)$$
$$G = G_0 \qquad (2.7)$$
$$X = X_0 \qquad (2.8)$$
$$M = mY \qquad (2.9)$$

It is assumed that b and m have a value between 0 and 1. A further reasonable assumption would be that tax, T, would also be a function of Y i.e.:

$$T = tY. \qquad (2.10)$$

Substituting (2.10) into (2.5) we therefore have:

$$C = a + b [Y - tY]$$

or

$$C = a + bY - btY \qquad (2.11)$$

and from (2.4):

$$Y = a + bY - btY + I_0 + G_0 + X_0 - mY$$

Collecting terms:

$$Y - bY + btY + mY = a + I_0 + G_0 + X_0$$

and factorizing and transposing:

$$Y = \frac{a + I_0 + G_0 + X_0}{1 - b + bt + m} \qquad (2.12)$$

The term $1/(1 - b + bt + m)$ is referred to as the multiplier and since it is greater than one, implies that any change in, say, government expenditure will

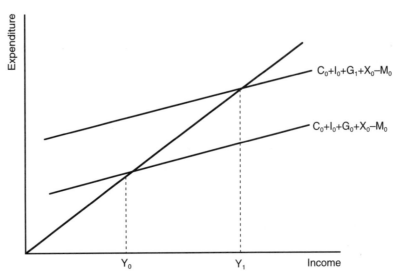

Figure 2.1 Effect of an increase in government expenditure

lead to a greater change in income as long as there are spare resources available.

The model is easily illustrated diagrammatically (Figure 2.1). Anywhere on the 45° line represents an equilibrium solution, Y_0 being a case in point, so that, if nothing else changes, that could be a stable equilibrium. There is no requirement for this to involve full employment, however. Keynes was writing just after the Great Depression and he had little faith in the classical belief that cuts in prices and wages would increase the profitability of firms and lead to increased output and more jobs at such times. His solution was an increase in government expenditure from G_0 to G_1 in the diagram which has the effect of shifting the aggregate demand curve upwards so that the new equilibrium results in higher income (and by inference employment). The same effect can be achieved by a reduction in taxes which would have the effect of swivelling the expenditure curve outwards from point A in Figure 2.2 assuming, as we are, that taxes are a function of income. The effect is, of course, an expansion of consumption from C_0 to C_1 for its slope is affected by the change in t. Refer to equation (2.11) to confirm this result. Note from Figure 2.1 that the change in $Y = \Delta Y$ is much greater than the change in $G = \Delta G$ which illustrates the multiplier.

The model has a number of defects the most important of which is that it ignores the possible impact of money and supply constraints in achieving desired levels of income. It is mainly relevant, therefore, to deep depressions. In practice supply constraints can be quite serious and may have contributed to the problem in the UK for much of the post-war period that full employment was not consistent with balance of payments equilibrium. Thus, in the 'stop-go' era of the 1950s and 1960s, governments would expand the economy to reduce unemployment and then retrench as soon as imports were sucked in when the balance of payments became negative. As the value of

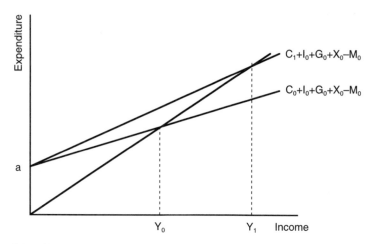

Figure 2.2 Effect of a cut in income tax

Box 2.4 The stability of the Keynesian consumption function

Though Keynes was correct in suggesting that consumption is a function of income, empirical evidence suggests that it is not a stable one. In the periods, 1974–76, 1979–82 and 1991–95 consumption was very much less than would have been predicted by the overall relationship from around 1980 onwards, whereas in the late 1980s, it was very much higher. Clearly, other factors are also important. One is uncertainty caused in the 1970s by oil price hikes and the consequent increases in unemployment. In the 1990s, the increase in unemployment, short-time and temporary working associated with the recession and the reduced value of perceived real wealth because of falling house prices were major influences. In the 1980s, on the other hand, falling unemployment, rising house prices and real incomes boosted both optimism and consumer spending. At the very least, therefore, expected future income and wealth need to be brought into the analysis as determinants of consumption.

---

the pound was fixed to other countries' exchange rates at that time, deflation rather than devaluation was normally the only solution to remedy excessive imports.

It appears, therefore, that we need to move on to more sophisticated models. We now consider the impact of supply constraints. Monetary constraints are examined in the appendix to this chapter.

Questions

1. Given the following structural equations:

$$C = a + b[Y - T]$$
$$X = X_0$$
$$G = G_0$$
$$I = I_0$$
$$T = T_0$$
$$M = mY$$

(a) Find the reduced form for income in equilibrium.
(b) How does income change in response to changes in:

   i) G, ii) T, iii) I, iv) X?

2. Given the following structural equations:

$$C = 20 + 0.9[Y - T]$$
$$I = 280$$
$$G = 510$$
$$T = 100 + 1/3\ Y$$
$$X = 180$$
$$M = 0.1Y$$

(a) What is the equilibrium level of national income?
(b) What is the Government fiscal surplus/deficit?
(c) What is the balance of payments surplus/deficit?
(d) What is the value of the multiplier?
(e) If X goes up by 30, what are the new answers to questions (a), (b) and (c)?
(f) If given the original figures both G and the fixed component of T rise by 100 (i.e. $T = 200 + 1/3\ Y$), what happens to equilibrium income?
(g) Assuming that the full employment level of output was 1920 what level of government spending would be necessary to raise output to that level?
(h) What is the impact of a change in the money supply or price level in this model.

3. What is the 'multiplier'? What is its significance for economic policy?
4. Given the model:

$$C = b[Y - T]$$
$$I = 200 + gY$$
$$T = tY$$
$$G = G_0$$
$$M = mY$$
$$X = X_0$$

and $C = 480$, $Y = 1000$, $T = 200$, $I = 300$, $M = 100$, $G = 240$, $X = 80$.

(a) Deduce the value of the parameters.
(b) What problems are revealed in this economy?
(c) How should they be solved?

2.3 THE AGGREGATE DEMAND–AGGREGATE SUPPLY MODEL

Aggregate demand

The simple Keynesian analysis of the model in section 2.2 excludes the impact of supply constraints and avoids the problem of price changes by specifying relationship in real terms. There are, however, a number of reasons why aggregate demand could be affected by price changes. First, a fall in prices, other things remaining equal means a rise in real money balances, a rise in the purchasing power of money and a likely rise in consumption. Those on fixed incomes might clearly be expected to spend more. Second, a fall in prices with a given money stock implies a fall in the demand for money and a reduced interest rate. That should mean an increase in investment. Finally, a reduction in the price of UK goods if unmatched abroad should lead to an increased demand for UK exports and a fall in imports. Of course, all this suggests far more sophisticated determinants of aggregate demand than those of the simple Keynesian model but implies in that model that a lower price level would shift the AD schedule upwards as shown in Figure 2.3.

Thus the fall in the price level from P_0 to P_1 increases equilibrium income from Y_0 to Y_1. This relationship is drawn in Figure 2.4.

An increase in government expenditure from G_0 to G_1 in Figure 2.3 will lead to an upward shift in the demand schedule at price level P_1 to AD_2. The effect in Figure 2.4 is a rightward shift in the AD curve with a new income level Y_2 at $P = P_1$. Any increase in the non-price determinants of aggregate demand will have the same effect and these determinants include autonomous investment, world trade and, as shown in the model in the appendix, the nominal money supply.

None of this is contentious but aggregate supply certainly is.

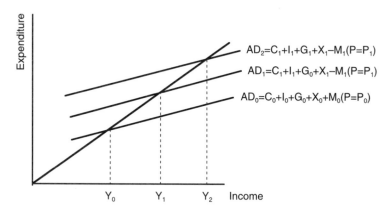

Figure 2.3 Implied effect of a fall in the price level

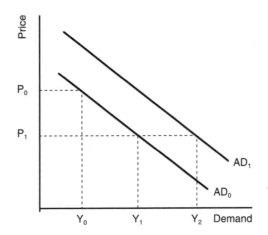

Figure 2.4 Aggregate demand curve

Aggregate supply

There are three scenarios here.

The classical case

This scenario is that aggregate supply is unaffected by changes in price. One possible reason is that increases in prices will simply increase wages in proportion, meaning that there will be no incentive for firms to increase output. This would be particularly true at high levels of employment. The classical case is shown in Figure 2.5.

The simple Keynesian case

The second scenario is that aggregate supply is horizontal suggesting that if producers think they can sell extra output at existing prices they will supply it. This situation is only likely to occur in deep depressions if at all (Figure 2.6).

The upward sloping case

This scenario, as the name implies, suggests that the true position is between the two extremes of the first and second scenarios, as in Figure 2.7. It is a truer reflection of Keynesian thought than the simple Keynesian model and can be justified on the grounds that if firms' marginal costs are rising, higher prices will be necessary to justify increased output.

The total picture

We can now bring aggregate demand and supply together and see what happens if the Government decides to increase spending. As shown in Figure 2.8, the increase in government expenditure, G, leads to a rightward shift in

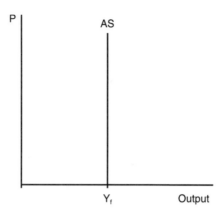

Figure 2.5 Vertical aggregate supply

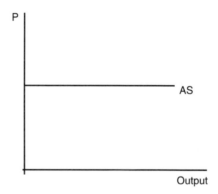

Figure 2.6 Horizontal aggregate supply

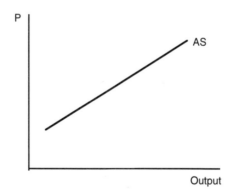

Figure 2.7 Upward sloping AS

the AD curve from AD_0 to AD_1. If the simple Keynesian supply curve (AS_1) applies we have a 'pure' output effect, an increase in income from Y_0 to Y_1, and no increase in the price level. If the upward-sloping case (AS_2) applies, output increases to Y_2 and the price level to P_1. Finally, if the vertical supply

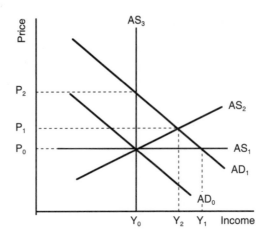

Figure 2.8 Effect of an increase in government spending

curve (AS_3) applies, there is a pure price effect from P_0 to P_2 and no increase in output. This is the same as the classical model in section 2.1 above.

The shape of the aggregate supply curve is, therefore, of crucial importance and is considered further in the next chapter. First, however, for those readers who would like to see the complete picture, the appendix examines a fourth model which explicitly considers monetary influences. This enables a more complete explanation of aggregate demand and supply, though the rest of the book can be read without it. For those readers avoiding the appendix it should be pointed out that increases in prices are often associated with rises in interest rates. Take for example an increase in government expenditure financed by borrowing rather than an increase in the money supply. The increased demand for funds is likely to directly increase interest rates. Any increase in prices given the unchanged money stock will add to the shortage of money and indirectly increase interest rates. As a result private investment may fall. This is referred to as 'crowding out'. More simply, rising prices means higher interest rates because the risk of lending money is greater. This is because it buys less goods when the loan is repaid.

APPENDIX: IS-LM ANALYSIS AND THE COMPLETE MODEL

The classical model is concerned with monetary influences and their effect on prices whereas the simple Keynesian model is concerned with the determination of *real* income (i.e. it is a volume or quantity determining model). The IS-LM model, model 4, has both a real and a monetary sector and enables us to examine monetary constraints. It also enables a more complete treatment of aggregate demand and supply. The model is generally regarded as being closer to what Keynes actually wrote in the General Theory (Keynes, 1936) than the model in section 2.2 above.

The real sector

This is the same as for the simple Keynesian model, i.e. in equilibrium:

$$Y = C + I + G + X - M \tag{2.13}$$

However, investment, I, is now assumed to partly depend on the rate of interest, that is,

$$I = i_0 - i_1 r \tag{2.14}$$

The effect of lower interest rates, therefore, is to increase investment and therefore given equation (2.4), aggregate demand. The new position is illustrated in (Figure 2.9) with the shift in the aggregate demand curve upwards from AD_0 to AD_1.

Thus falling rates of interest are associated with higher levels of real income given spare capacity. This is easily demonstrated using simple algebra. As in the previous model we have:

$$C = a + b\,(Y - T)$$
$$M = mY$$
$$X = X_0$$
$$G = G_0$$
$$T = tY$$

So the effect of the new investment function (2.14) is the new reduced form:

$$Y = \frac{a + G_0 + i_0 + X_0 - i_1 r}{1 - b + bt + m} \tag{2.15}$$

The model focuses on the relationship between equilibrium income and interest rates and as can be seen that relationship is negative, that is, *increases* in interest rates are associated with *reductions* in real income. The curve

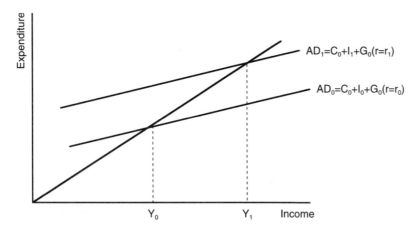

Figure 2.9 Effect of a fall in interest rates

plotting this relationship is typically referred to as the IS curve (drawn in Figure 2.10).

$$\text{The slope of the curve} = \frac{-i_1}{1 - b + bt + m} \tag{2.16}$$

where one divided by the denominator is, as before, the multiplier.

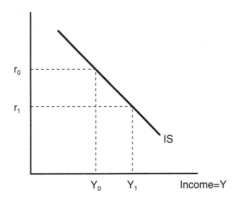

Figure 2.10 The IS curve

Shifts in the IS curve

The IS curve shifts in response to any change in the autonomous components of spending. A rise in government spending G, for example, leads to higher levels of income at all interest rates. Thus in Figure 2.11, the rise in G from G_0 to G_1 shifts the AD curve upwards (part (a)) and shifts the IS curve to the right (part (b)). The change in G times the multiplier gives the total horizontal shift in income.

The slope of the IS curve

As can be seen from equation (2.16), the steepness of the curve depends on how sensitive investment is to changes in the interest rate and also on the value of the multiplier. Thus if investment is sensitive to changes in r, then the IS curve is flat. Similarly, the higher the value of the multiplier the flatter the IS curve. As will be seen, the shape of the curve turns out be important.

  We now turn to the monetary sector of the model.

The monetary sector

Equilibrium in this sector requires that the real demand for money = the real supply of money.

  The real demand for money $\frac{M_D}{P}$ is assumed to be positively related to real income and inversely related to the rate of interest i.e.:

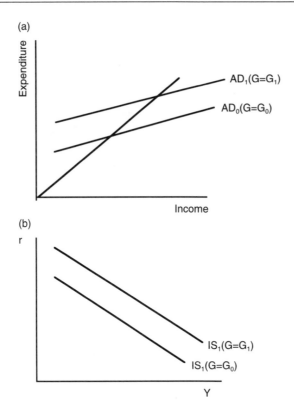

Figure 2.11 parts (a) and (b) Aggregate demand and the IS curve

$$\frac{M_D}{P} = l_1 Y - l_2 r$$

(2.17)

The justification is as follows.

Higher real income will mean more money demanded since it implies higher spending on goods and services. This explains the first part of the right-hand side of (2.17). The other part is explained by the fact that a high interest rate means that holding cash as opposed to opening a deposit account or buying bonds means significant loss of potential interest. Economists refer to this loss as the **opportunity cost** of holding cash and the higher interest rates are, the less people will be prepared to accept it.

The relationship between $\frac{M_D}{P}$ and r is depicted in Figure 2.12. An increased level of income shifts the curve to the right.

The real money supply (at least for now) may be regarded as autonomous:

$$\frac{M_S}{P} = \frac{M_0}{P}$$

(2.18)

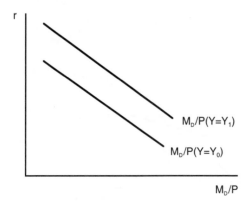

Figure 2.12 The shift in demand for money

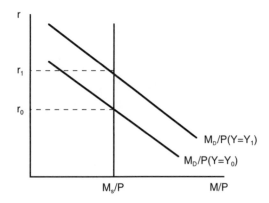

Figure 2.13 Effect of an increase in income

This is shown by the vertical line in Figure 2.13. In equilibrium $\frac{M_S}{P}$ must equal $\frac{M_D}{P}$. Clearly if real income rises this has to mean increased rates of interest from r_0 to r_1.

Algebraically, we have:

$$\frac{M_D}{P} = \frac{M_S}{P} = l_1 Y - l_2 r$$

Rearranging we have:

$$Y = \frac{(M_S/P) + l_2 r}{l_1} \tag{2.19}$$

This gives us the relationship between real income and the rate of interest as far as the monetary sector is concerned. As can be seen from (2.19) this is positive, the slope being $= (l_2/l_1)$. This relationship is depicted in the so-called LM curve of Figure 2.14.

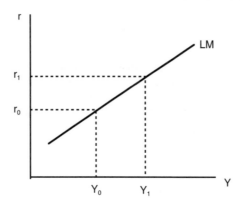

Figure 2.14 The LM curve

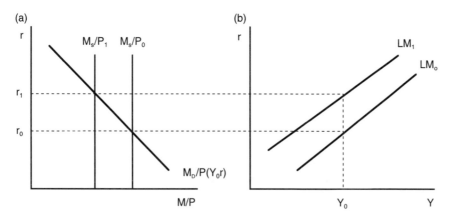

Figure 2.15 parts (a) and (b) Effect of an increase in the price level

Shifts in the LM curve

The LM curve shifts if the price level shifts or if the nominal money supply changes – the effect is the same. An increase in P, for example, shifts the real money supply M_S/P to the left (Figure 2.15). This leads to an equilibrium at a higher interest rate and the same level of income. Similarly, an increase in the nominal money supply M_S would shift the LM curve to the right because a lower interest rate would now be associated with a constant level of real income.

Slope of the LM curve

From equation 2.19, the more the responsiveness of the demand for money to income (l_1) and *the lower the responsiveness of the demand for money to the interest rate l_2*, the steeper is the LM curve. This also turns out to be an important issue.

Simultaneous equilibrium

This is given by the intersection of the IS and LM curves as shown in Figure 2.16. The diagram illustrates the solution to the model. This is in real terms, it being assumed for the present that the price level does not vary. The model indicates that both fiscal policy and/or monetary policy can be used to stimulate aggregate demand. It should be pointed out that there is no consideration of supply constraints.

Fiscal policy

The effect of **fiscal policy** such as an increase in government expenditure is to shift the IS curve to the right (Figure 2.17). It should be noted that the increase in income ($Y_1 - Y_0$) is less than that of the simple Keynesian model (= $Y_2 - Y_0$). The reason is that the expansion of output raises interest rates which partially 'crowd out' private investment. Monetary constraints are, therefore, of some importance. Of course, fiscal policy will be more effective the *flatter* is the LM curve. Keynesians tend to take the view that it is relatively flat and, therefore, advocate *fiscal* approaches to policy problems.

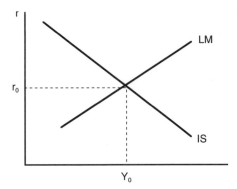

Figure 2.16 Intersection of IS and LM curves

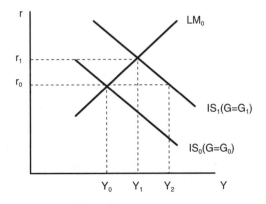

Figure 2.17 Impact of increased government expenditure

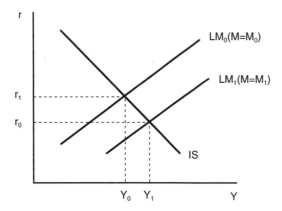

Figure 2.18 Impact of monetary expansion

Monetary policy

The effect of an expansionary **monetary policy** is to shift the LM curve to the right, as shown in Figure 2.18. The result is an increase in income and a reduction in interest rates which will be more affective the flatter is the IS curve. Monetarists tend to take the view that it is relatively flat and advocate *monetary* approaches to policy problems.

Both scenarios, however, assume, as above, that prices are fixed. This is equivalent to saying that the model refers exclusively to aggregate demand (AD). Supply (AS) must be passive or increased demand would drive up the price of factors and the price of goods, and shift the LM curve to the left. This is a more likely scenario as we shall now see from our re-examination of aggregate demand and supply.

Questions

1. Given the equations for an economy with no foreign trade:

$$Y = C + I$$
$$C = a + bY$$
$$I = i_0 - i_1 r$$

$$\frac{M_D}{P} = l_1 Y - l_2 r$$

$$\frac{M_S}{P} = \frac{M_D}{P}$$

    derive the IS and LM curves.

2. (a) What is meant by 'crowding out'? Demonstrate diagrammatically by use of the IS-LM model.

(b) If complete 'crowding out' occurred what would be the shape of the LM curve?

(c) Can cuts in government spending 'crowd in' private sector expenditures?

3. Assuming a two sector economy with no foreign trade and no government sector where:

$$Y = C + I$$
$$C = 48 + 0.8Y$$
$$I = 98 - 75r$$
$$M_S/P = 248$$
$$M_D/P = 0.3Y + 5 - 150r$$
$$P = 1$$

find the equilibrium values of Y, r, C, I, M_S and M_D.

4. Using the IS-LM model distinguish the effects of fiscal and monetary policy on interest rates and output.

The aggregate demand–aggregate supply model reconsidered

This allows for price changes affecting aggregate demand and supply, the latter having so far been ignored.

Aggregate demand

The equation for the LM curve contains price.

$$Y = \frac{M/P + l_2 r}{l_1} \tag{2.20}$$

As was seen above, an increase in P leads to a reduction in the real money supply which shifts the LM curve to the left. The increase in interest rates reduces endogenous investment and income falls. It follows that increases in prices lead to a fall in aggregate demand. This is shown in Figure 2.19 in the reduction in aggregate demand from Y_0 to Y. This is plotted against the price level in the bottom half of the diagram.

For simplicity, the IS curve is assumed here to be based on real influences and if so would be unaffected by changes in P. In the above diagram, the increase in the price level shifts LM to the left, interest rates rise to r_1 and income falls to Y_1. As argued in the main text, the AD curve will shift if any of the non-price factors change. Given the three aggregate supply curve scenarios also itemized in the main text we can now examine the impact of an increase in government expenditure in our complete model.

The complete model

This is shown in Figure 2.20, which adds the supply-side to the simple IS/LM model. We start at the intersection of LM_1 and IS_0 with an equilibrium income

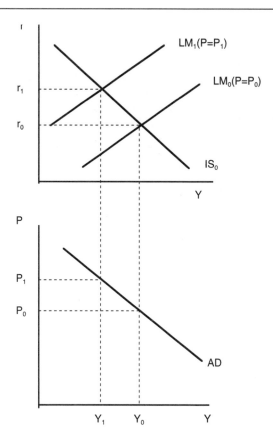

Figure 2.19 Derivation of AD curve

level Y_0. Assume an increase in government expenditure. This shifts the IS curve to the right. In the absence of monetary factors this would increase income to Y_3, as in the model in section 2.2. The rise in demand, however, drives up interest rates and results in the rise in income being moderated to Y_2. This is the IS-LM case of model 4. What then happens depends on our assumptions about AS:

1. If AS is horizontal, income = Y_2 and the conclusion of model 4 applies.
2. If AS is upward-sloping, an increase in output can only be secured at higher prices. Higher prices reduce the real value of the money supply, LM shifts to LM_2 and output = Y_1. The new intersection is at Y_1 given by the intersection of AD_1 and AS_2, in the bottom half of the diagram and by the intersection of LM_2 and IS_1 in the top half.
3. If AS is vertical, the increase in demand causes increases in prices to P_2, and interest rates to r_3 and leaves output unaffected at Y_0. Recent theory, as will be seen below, has essentially the same result, which corresponds with the model in section 2.1. In this case, only supply-side factors can increase employment.

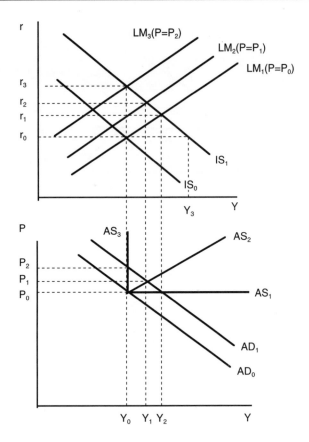

Figure 2.20 The complete model

This model, therefore, shows the interaction between interest rates, prices and output and is a basis for the analysis of economic forecasting models and economic policies. From now on, we concentrate on the bottom part of Figure 2.20.

Schools of thought 3

We know what happens to people who stay in the middle of the road. They get run over.

(Aneurin Bevan)

In economics there is little controversy about aggregate demand but considerable debate on aggregate supply. Though there are many shades of opinion it will be convenient to group them into three main schools of thought. These are monetarist, new classical and Keynesian and to highlight the essential differences we examine the aggregate supply curve in more detail.

3.1 AGGREGATE SUPPLY

As argued in the last chapter, aggregate supply reflects what firms in total would wish to supply given changes in the underlying determinants. The classical view, that the curve is vertical, is based upon a particular perception of the labour market. Employment is determined in that view by the intersection of labour demand and supply schedules both of which are assumed to be a function of the real wage. This is illustrated in Figure 3.1. The upward-sloping labour supply curve shows that as existing workers are offered a higher real wage they will work more hours while some potential workers will now be persuaded to join the labour force.

The labour supply curve will shift to the right as the population of working age increases and as welfare benefits fall relative to wages. The downward-sloping labour demand curve is a consequence of the assumption that firms

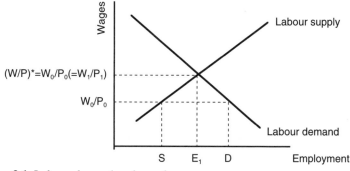

Figure 3.1 Labour demand and supply

maximize profits. The revenue earned by a worker is equal to his output (per year) multiplied by the price (P) of that output. As nominal wages (W) fall, for a fixed price level, that is, real wages (W/P) fall, the workers 'price themselves into jobs', earning more profit (per person) for the firm. Firms therefore increase their demand for labour; the labour demand schedule is downward-sloping. The labour demand curve *shifts* to the right as the productivity of labour increases (e.g. as better capital equipment is installed).

In the classical model there will be some unemployment at an employment level E_1. However, this is frictional or voluntary unemployment, as workers change jobs and search for better job offers. Employment tends to return to E_1 in this model because wages and prices are assumed to be *perfectly flexible*. Hence, if we are momentarily at a lower real wage, W_0/P_1, the demand for labour D exceeds the supply S. Hence, firms bid for workers and raise their wage offers to W_1. As they do so the real wages rise back to W_1/P_1 $(= W_0/P_0)$. Demand for labour falls and supply rises, so that they are again equal at E^1. Prices and wages rise by equal amounts because of 'bidding' in the market (i.e. firms advertise 'new' job vacancies and readvertise 'old' job vacancies at higher wage rates). At the wage (W_1/P_1) all workers who *wish to work* at this real wage rate do so; any unemployment is voluntary.

The final strand in the classical view of the supply-side is that firms simultaneously produce more output as new workers are hired and, therefore, if employment stays at E_1 then output will also remain at its full employment (or natural) rate which is depicted as Y_f in Figure 3.2. The supply curve in Figure 3.2 is vertical because as prices rise (as described above) wages are bid up so that the real wage stays at $(W/P)^*$ and employment and hence output remain at E_1 and Y_f respectively.

The latter scenario occurs because workers do *not* suffer from 'money' illusion and realize that higher prices reduce their purchasing power. Higher prices would be met by higher wage demands so that profit margins (i.e. prices over wage costs) would remain constant and manufacturers have no incentive to raise output in response to their higher prices.

What might cause a shift in AS? Clearly *shifts* in the underlying supply and

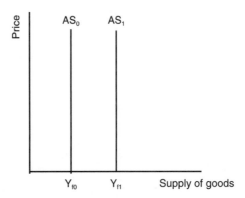

Figure 3.2 The vertical aggregate supply curve

demand for labour curves yield a new equilibrium level of employment and
hence a new level of output. Therefore, a fall in welfare benefits or a cut in
income tax rates which shifts the labour supply curve rightwards or a rise in
labour productivity which shifts the labour demand curve to the right will
increase the equilibrium or 'natural' rate of employment and output as classical economists like to call it. In Figure 3.2, AS shifts from AS_0 to AS_1.

There are, however, reasons why the aggregate supply curve may not be
vertical. Such a situation would occur if the rising prices increased the
perceived profitability of producing more goods (i.e. the profit margin over
wage costs P/W increased or, equivalently, the real wage W/P fell). This
would happen if selling prices rose more than production costs because:

- workers were interested in money rather than real wages;
- workers' expectations of the price level lagged behind its actual value;
- institutional factors stopped wages increasing as fast as prices.

Clearly, if some of these factors are true in the short-run rather than the long
then we have the possibility of different long- and short-run aggregate supply
curves. This situation is depicted in Figure 3.3.

Thus a shift in AD from AD_0 to AD_1 may result in an increase in output if
workers fail to realize the extent to which prices are rising, or if they are
temporarily 'locked' into wage agreements. They therefore supply more in
response to rising or constant money wages (but falling *real* wages) and we
move from point A to point B on the short-term supply curve SAS_0. Workers
cannot, however, be duped in the long-run and eventually they choose to
supply less labour at the current (new) price level P_1. The result is a shift in
the short-run curve to SAS_1 and a movement to C. The long-run curve joins
points of equilibrium such as A and C, though even that may not be vertical.

The main points of contention concern this issue and also the length of
time involved in the long and short-run. We now examine these issues
further by examining in turn monetarist, rational expectations and Keynesian
perspectives.

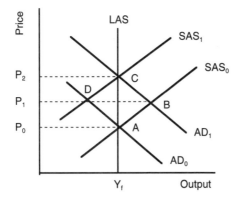

Figure 3.3 Long- and short-run equilibria

3.2 MONETARISTS

The essence of the orthodox monetarist position is that any expansion of aggregate demand by, for example, an increase in the money supply (in excess of growth in real output) or an increase in government expenditure is likely to affect only prices in the long-run. Thus, we would eventually move from point A to point C with output remaining at Y_f. This 'natural' rate of output, as argued in the previous section, is determined by the productive potential of the economy. This in turn is determined by labour productivity and the position of the labour demand curve in Figure 3.1. More capital equipment or improved managerial and working practices can slowly increase labour productivity, move the demand for labour outwards and hence also move the LAS curve to the right.

Because the money supply only influences prices in the long-run this is known as the **neutrality proposition**. The fact that government expenditure does *not* influence output in the long-run is known as (complete) **crowding out.**

Orthodox monetarists recognize that there may, however, be short-run effects which mean that the process of adjustment from one long-run equilibrium (at A) to another (at C) may be complicated and unpredictable (Figure 3.3). They envisage a movement to B as firms and workers make mistakes in anticipating the (general) rise in prices. Therefore, firms overestimate expected profits and wish to supply more goods, and workers overestimate the purchasing power of their nominal wages and are willing to produce more. For example, suppose SAS_0 reflects what would be supplied given an expected price level of P_0. The actual price level rise to P_1 given the shift in AD and the movement from A to B, and expectations will now change given the new observed price level. In other words, workers learn from their past errors and in future periods they recognize that in terms of the goods they can purchase they are less well off. Hence, they supply less labour and, therefore, output at the new level of prices P_1. Thus the SAS curve shifts to the left and towards a new equilibrium at C. The path of adjustment may not be smooth, however, and could well involve overshooting if expectations do not adjust smoothly. In this case, the movement of output might be as indicated by the dotted line in Figure 3.4.

In this scenario, expansions of aggregate demand are destablizing and produce cycles in output. A further tenet of monetarist thought is that though such cycles can also occur due to random supply shocks (e.g. an oil price increase affecting all firms), governments are not equipped to attempt to redress them.

Monetarists, therefore, advocate that the expansion of the money supply should merely accommodate the underlying long-term growth rate of real output in the economy as set by productivity increases. The essence of their position is that such growth can only occur in the long-run because of a shift in the LAS curve and that these shifts occur *independently* of demand.

It is perhaps worth looking at the reverse case (Figure 3.3). Given the

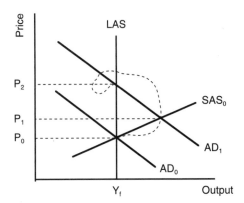

Figure 3.4 The monetarist view

monetarist position, a reduction in AD from AD_1 to AD_0 should move the economy from C to D in the short-run and to A in the long-run.

Critics would argue that the long-run may be very long and that the movement from D to A can be speeded up by government policy changes. Indeed empirical work (Tobin, 1981) suggests that the neutrality result may take ten to fifteen years to fully work through the economy. Over this period, the underlying behavioural relationships are very likely to have changed. Critics also point out that the money supply is difficult to control even on an annual basis.

3.3   The New Classical School (NC)

The new classical school may be regarded as extreme monetarist. There are two elements in the approach of its adherents. First, they believe that economic agents will make *efficient* use of all available information on the variable about which expectations are formed. They are assumed to act as if they used a model (in their head) for forecasting and these forecasts form the basis of their expectations about, for example, the exchange rate or prices. Hence their expectations are *consistent* with the predictions of their own macro model. These are called 'rational expectations', RE. Thus, if people believe that a change in the money supply affects the price level, they will use information on the money supply to predict prices. The second strand in their argument is that all prices are perfectly flexible so that markets clear immediately in all periods. These two elements taken together imply a much sharper process of adjustment than for orthodox monetarism, at least for those circumstances when a credible policy change is announced in advance.

It should be pointed out however, that RE can also be applied in models where prices are sluggish (sticky) and these models do not produce the 'extreme' new classical results described below. This will be demonstrated in later chapters when issues such as exchange rate overshooting are discussed.

The essence of the NC position can be illustrated by assuming, for example, that the Government *announces* a higher money supply target for next year and are believed. This is indicated by an anticipated shift in AD from AD_0 to AD_1 in Figure 3.3. Economic agents know that the increase in the money supply is to occur and also know that this will affect prices and produce a new equilibrium at C. Since they are 'rational' they immediately adjust expectations and we move straight from A to C.

In this scenario, there are no short-run effects on output from an *anticipated* change in the money supply. On the other hand even the NC school recognizes that an *unanticipated* increase in the money supply will have effects on output in the very short-run. This is because suppliers of output are 'surprised' by the price increase and see that more sales are temporarily profitable at the higher prices (but fixed wages) and hence expand output along SAS_0. However, this move from A to B is either very quickly reversed if the money supply falls back to its original level or the economy *quickly* moves to C if the increase in the money supply turns out to be permanent. The NC school, therefore, makes a clear distinction between the effects of *anticipated* and *unanticipated* changes in policy variables.

It should be emphasized that the authorities cannot keep on randomly increasing the money supply to expand output. Rational agents will recognize this fact and the initially *unanticipated* increase will become *anticipated* and then it will affect only prices and not output.

An important point about NC is that it seems to offer a simple solution to inflation. If the rate of inflation is considered too high, all that needs to be done is to announce a reduction in the money supply which must be credible.

If expectations adjust immediately there will be no effects on output. Thus in static terms a cut in AD from AD_1 to AD_0 (Figure 3.3) immediately takes us from C to a new price level of P_0 at point A. Of crucial importance here, of course, is the credibility of the announcement. Thus some NC protagonists favour 'cold turkey' (i.e. a large announced cut in the money supply) rather than the orthodox monetarist gradualist approach. The former, it is argued, has more impact on expectations because it is a clear break with a previous policy stance.

In addition to the criticisms of orthodox monetarism it may be argued against NC/RE that:

- most people have neither the knowledge nor the economic expertise to be rational (although we only require those 'on the margin' to be rational for the theory to be valid);
- expectations are slow to adjust because agents must learn about their new environment and RE has no model of learning behaviour;
- some prices are 'sticky'; thus although the NC approach may be usefully applied to financial and FOREX markets, it should not be applied to labour and goods markets.

3.4 KEYNESIANS

The essence of the Keynesian position is that instability is endemic to capitalist economies and that the manipulation of aggregate demand is needed to prevent recurrent crises. Furthermore, aggregate demand and supply are not independent and there may be no automatic adjustment to full employment. Again, Figure 3.3 may be used to illustrate the latter Keynesian views. Assume that we begin at point A with output Y_f and that policy-makers wish to expand output. Thus they use monetary or fiscal policy to shift AD from AD_0 to AD_1 and we again move to point B on SAS_0. The problem is to stay there and Keynesians would argue that if the economy can be held long enough at B, the LAS would begin to shift to the right. This could be because the higher levels of demand would increase business confidence, investment and the productivity of the economy so that potential output was higher. Thus, increases in aggregate demand may generate an appropriate supply response particularly, as some of the long-term unemployed would get jobs and display the characteristics of employability. The simplest case would be the situation depicted in Figure 3.5 and a permanent movement to point B. In practice, the short-run supply curve would also probably shift and the LAS curve may not shift as far as B so that a more realistic result would be point C on SAS_1 and LAS_2.

It should be emphasized that this applies in reverse too. Thus, if we begin at point C in Figure 3.3 with an employment level Y_f and attempt to reduce the price level to P_0 we in fact tend to end up at a point like D. In this case, the LAS curve shifts to the left and business confidence is eroded, as expectations do not adjust and as many of those tainted by unemployment become unemployable.

So are the Keynesians right? There probably are many institutional reasons (such as wage contracts) which do mean that the short-run supply curve shifts slowly in response to a shift in demand. However, it does shift, which is one reason why Keynesians advocate incomes policies. Such policies have not been markedly successful when used in the UK. Also as far as the UK is

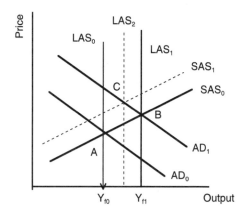

Figure 3.5 A Keynesian view

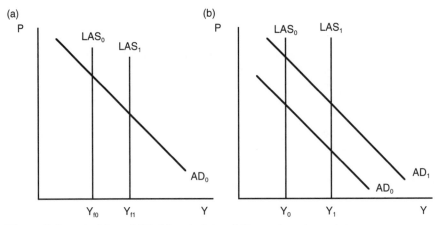

Figure 3.6 parts (a) and (b) Monetarist and Keynesian viewpoints

concerned, the problem is one of getting a sufficient supply-side response to shift the LAS curve to the right. In practice, increases in AD have quickly filtered into imports and this is a reason why some Keynesians advocate import controls. In any event, it is clear that the supply-side is as important to Keynesians as to monetarists. The difference is that manipulation of demand is also important in the Keynesian case.

Thus to sum up, the main difference between monetarists and Keynesians is that, in the monetarist case, tinkering with demand has no long-run effect on supply while, in the Keynesian case, governments may have to give a boost to demand in certain circumstances to get an appropriate supply-side response. This difference is illustrated in Figures 3.6 (a) and (b).

A situation when Keynesian economics may be applicable is, of course, in deep depressions when, due to a deficiency of aggregate demand, the labour market does not clear in the manner suggested by the classical economists.

3.5 Conclusion

There are, then, a number of important differences in perception among groups of economists as to how the economy operates. The important differences concern the use of rational expectations, the operation of the supply-side of the economy and whether an increase in aggregate demand is needed to boost that supply-side. Though there has been a narrowing of differences in recent years with Keynesians in particular accepting the importance of supply-side policies to boost economic growth, substantial differences remain as will be evident in subsequent chapters. First, we make our analysis a little more realistic by looking at changes in prices rather than the price level.

Box 3.1 Reformation, counter-reformation and counter-counter reformation?

> The Keynesian revolution was a revolt against the traditional modes of thought about the economy, and monetarism was a counter-revolution to reassert them.
>
> (Pratten, 1990)

The classical view was that resources including labour would be fully utilized in the long run. To Keynes, writing during the Great Depression of the 1930s when unemployment had reached one in three of the work-force in some parts of the country, this was not terribly reassuring. His famous dictum was that 'in the long run we are all dead'. As far as Keynes was concerned the self-adjusting properties of the economy were weak and deficiency of aggregate demand had to be corrected by increases in goverment spending. The obvious inference is that at times of excess aggregate demand the opposite should apply.

There is no doubt that increased goverment spending associated with the 'New Deal' in America and rearmament in Europe were instrumental in the recovery from the mid-1930s onwards and Keynesian ideas influenced policy-makers until the start of the 1970s. By that time, the emergence of high inflation *and* increasing levels of unemployment led to a breakdown in the Keynesian belief in counter-cyclical or stabilization policy and in the view that goverments could secure low levels of unemployment over the long term, Monetarists such as Milton Friedman argued that economies were inherently unstable and that attempts to operate counter-cyclically would exacerbate the underlying problems. Governments simply did not know enough about economies to engage in 'fine tuning' and information and administrative lags guaranteed that by the time policy was operating it was too late. Thus a boost to aggregate demand would only become effective after the economy was already picking up, thereby magnifying a developing boom. Moreover, Friedman argued that attempts to increase the level of aggregate demand were the main cause of developing high inflation. To him, economic policy should be largely confined to keeping the growth of the money supply to the rate of growth of productivity. This turned out to be impossible as monetary targets were repeatedly missed.

Extreme new classical monetarists went further, believing that rational expectations held and that deregulated competitive markets would quickly adjust to random shocks. Government interventionist policy was pointless because rational economic agents would change their behaviour to allow for it. As a result, policy intervention could only have an impact in the short run, and then only if it was unanticipated.

Failure to control the money supply, competitive deflation, prolonged high unemployment and low rates of economic growth in Europe and America have begun to cause a reappraisal. The British government no longer targets broad monetary aggregates and there is an increasing belief that govern-ments must do something more about high rates of unemployment than simply relying on training schemes, reduced welfare payments and similar supply-side measures. A cynic would argue that monetarism and monetarist presciptions failed in the 1930s and that the lessons of history were not learnt. Equally, however, the very low levels of unemployment achieved in the 1960s were ultimately unsustainable. That is another historical lesson.

Questions

1. How is the long-run defined in the monetarist analysis of aggregate supply?
2. What is meant by the proposition that money is neutral?
3. Why, to monetarists, is the short-run aggregate supply curve upward-sloping while the long-run aggregate supply curve is vertical? Do shifts in the aggregate supply curve depend solely on technological innovation and productivity?
4. Explain the term 'rational expectations'.
5. What factors determine whether an increase in aggregate demand will lead to an increase in prices or output?
6. What are the essential differences between a) classical and new classical economists, and b) monetarists and Keynesians?
7. Which group of economists believe in stabilization policy?
8. (a) Given an aggregate demand curve

   $$AD_0 = 128 - 9P$$

   a short-run aggregate supply curve

   $$SAS_0 = 7P - 32$$

   and a long-run curve $LAS_0 = 38$, find the equilibrium short- and long-run price and output.
   (b) If there is an increase in the money supply so that we have a new AD curve

   $$AD_1 = 144 - 9P$$

   what is the new short-run equilibrium?
   (c) If, in the long-run, we have a new SAS curve

   $$SAS_1 = 7P - 44.45$$

   is money approximately neutral?
   (d) Keynesians would hope that the LAS curve would shift in response to the increasein the money supply. Write an expression for a new LAS curve consistent with the equilibrium between SAS_0 and AD_1.

Inflation 4

Inflation is everywhere and always a monetary phenomenon.

(Milton Friedman)

The analysis so far has been concerned with levels of output, wages, prices and the money supply whereas in practice economists are much more likely to be concerned with *changes* in the levels. One particularly important issue is the rate of inflation which can be analysed fairly simply by extending the analysis of the previous two chapters.

4.1 CHANGES

It was argued in Chapters 2 and 3 that aggregate demand was negatively related to the level of prices and a mainstream view would be that the

---

Box 4.1 The retail price index

This is used to measure the rate of inflation in the UK and is based upon the cost of a representative basket of goods and services bought by a typical household. The procedure is to select the list of items to be included in the index and to ascribe them weights according to their importance in family expenditure. The latter is assessed from the annual Family Expenditure Survey based on the responses of around 7,000 households chosen to represent all types and all UK regions. Weights and items are updated on an annual basis. The prices of the respective items are collated on a month to month basis from a representative range of retail outlets, the average being used. The overall weighted average price is expressed as an index on the base year which is currently 1987. Recent details are given below:

Table 4.1 UK retail price index (1987 = 100)

1991	133.5
1992	138.5
1993	140.7
1994	144.7
1995	149.1

Source: Office for National Statistics (1996), p. T26

aggregate supply curve is upward-sloping in the short-run and (more controversially) vertical in the long-run. These relationships are depicted in Figure 4.1, where LAS and SAS are the long- and short-run supply curves.

It is possible to redraw Figure 4.1 with the rate of inflation, on the vertical axis. The reason is that, at any given time, an increase in the inflation rate ensures a higher price level than there would otherwise have been. The implied relationship between inflation and output is shown in Figure 4.2. Of course, these are not the same curves as in Figure 4.1 and for that reason the prefix D is used to show that they reflect the *dynamic* relationship between p and output.

The point Y_0 is defined in monetarist and new classical parlance as the natural rate of output. It is natural in the sense that it is the rate at which aggregate supply equals aggregate demand in the long-run. We now show why. For simplicity, assume that in the absence of productivity growth the monetarists are correct in believing that in the long-run the rate of change of prices will be equal to the rate of change of the money supply. Assume that this is 12 per cent and that we begin in equilibrium at point A in Figure 4.3.

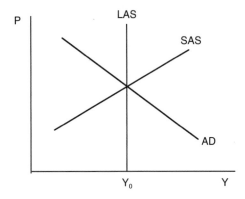

Figure 4.1 Aggregate demand and supply as a function of the price level

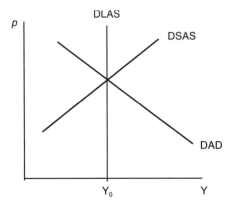

Figure 4.2 Aggregate demand and supply as a function of the rate of inflation

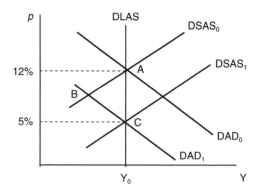

Figure 4.3 The level of output

Let us now assume that the Government feels that 12 per cent is too high a rate of inflation and cuts the money supply growth rate to 5 per cent. As the growth of the money stock is now lower than the rate of inflation, the purchasing power of the money stock falls, people feel less wealthy and the aggregate demand curve shifts to the left. It falls, in fact, until it cuts the DLAS curve at 5 per cent, for if it did not there would be a fall in the purchasing power of the money stock and we would be unable to maintain demand at Y_0. Thus inflation has to fall to 5 per cent to restore equilibrium in the long-run.

The problem is that, even in monetarist models, we do not move straight to a point like C, but instead move down the short-run DSAS curve to point B. What happens there depends upon workers and their expectations. At point B inflation has fallen, but so has output and this implies an increase in unemployment. If there is a natural rate of unemployment, U_0, corresponding to the natural rate of output, Y_0, unemployment is now above the natural rate. In theory, what should now happen is that the real wage should fall, that firms' profits should, therefore, rise and that they will therefore wish to supply more; i.e. the short-run aggregate supply, DSAS, shifts to the right (to $DSAS_1$). Equilibrium is reached at point C, as illustrated in Figure 4.3. Should this occur, the outcome is permanently lower inflation at the expense of temporarily higher unemployment.

There are questions as to whether this process does occur, and if it does, the length of time it takes to move from B to C. This will depend upon the following factors:

1. Inflationary expectations. The quicker these adjust, the lower money wage demands and hence real wages will be. The lower the latter are, the lower firms' costs will be and the more they may wish to supply. In rational expectations models the process of adjustment would be almost immediate if the cut in the money supply was correctly perceived by the private sector.
2. Real wages. The more responsive these are to higher unemployment,

the faster firms' costs should fall and the quicker output supplied increases.

3. The extent to which firms do increase output as a result of a fall in costs, particularly given that falling levels of demand may affect business confidence. Even if costs do fall, firms may wish to wait and see before taking on more labour, thereby worsening the situation.

In practice, doubt may be cast upon the extent to which each of the above will occur, so that the economy may be locked at a point like B for a considerable time. Business lost is not easily regained and closed-down factories are not easily reopened, therefore, output may stay low for so long that some workers become unemployable. The result is that potential or natural output and the DLAS curve shift back towards point B.

In any event, as the UK evidence shows, economies can get stuck for considerable periods at points like B, suggesting that monetarist remedies for inflation are far less simple than originally supposed and also that, in certain circumstances, stimulation of demand may be beneficial. The latter is of course a Keynesian perspective.

There are perhaps two issues that we should explore further.

4.2 An Expansion of Aggregate Demand

Assume we begin at point C in Figure 4.4 and that the Government decides that the level of unemployment, U_0, corresponding to Y_0 is too high. It therefore expands demand by an increase in the growth of the money supply. We now move to a point D on $DSAS_0$. If the monetarists are correct, the curve will then begin to shift to the left and unemployment will start to rise again. The only way the Government can stop this is to keep expanding the money supply, so we move to a point E on the new DSAS curve, $DSAS_1$ (and new DAD curve DAD_2).

The net result, of course, is accelerating inflation. It follows, therefore, that attempts to keep unemployment below the natural rate cause permanently

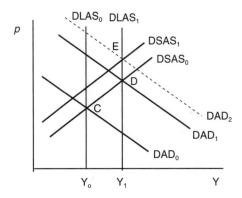

Figure 4.4 An expansion of aggregate demand

accelerating inflation in the monetarist view. For these reasons U_0 (corresponding to Y_0) is described as the non-accelerating inflation rate of unemployment, NAIRU. As we argued in Chapter 3, a shift in DLAS to $DLAS_1$ (through D) is an alternative possibility and this requires vigorous supply-side policies such as tax incentives, improved training, infrastructure and productivity. Keynesians might, therefore, support such policies in conjunction with the original government boost to aggregate demand.

4.3 A RISE IN NON-WAGE COSTS

A case in point here is the oil price rise of the early 1970s, which increased firms' costs and reduced profits in the non-oil exporting countries. If we return to Figure 4.3 and assume we start at C on DAD_1 and $DSAS_1$ this is depicted by a movement from C to B, as firms wish to supply less at a given rate of inflation. Two possibilities now exist for a return to Y_0. One is for a fall in wage costs to mitigate against the rise in oil costs so that DSAS shifts back to C. A second is that, in these circumstances, a government should expand aggregate demand so that we end up at point A. The inflationary costs are higher in the latter circumstance, but it may be argued that a quicker return to the natural rate of output–employment is thereby ensured.

4.4 IMPORTED INFLATION

This outlines the theoretical determination of prices and shows their inter-relationship with fiscal and monetary policy acting via changes in aggregate demand in a closed economy model. In practice, inflation can also be imported. Basically the problem is the price of imports which can go up, in domestic currency terms, either because the exchange rate has depreciated or because prices quoted in foreign currency terms have gone up. A general model of inflation would, therefore, have to encompass these effects and one which does is equation (4.1).

$$p = B_0(Y - Y_0) + B_1 p^e + B_2(p^* - s) \tag{4.1}$$

Thus inflation in this monetarist type of model would be a function of whether output was above its natural level (i.e. $Y > Y_0$), of inflationary expectations (p^e) and the change in the exchange rate (s).

4.5 CONCLUSION

This completes our analysis of the theoretical foundations and we will return to them from time to time in due course. We now move on to the analysis of macroeconomic risk and what, from a business perspective, can be done about it.

Box 4.2 Hysterisis effects

As argued in the text, monetarists believe in the concept of a *natural* rate of output, employment and unemployment determined in the long run by the productive potential of the economy. The natural rate corresponds with the NAIRU, the non-accelerating inflation rate of unemployment. Thus, if output is at the natural level, there should be no tendency for inflation to change, since expectations will have adjusted such that the actual rate of inflation will equal the expected rate. Unfortunately, if there is a natural rate of output and unemployment, it seems to be very variable. Unemployment in the UK in 1973 was around 3 per cent after which it rose to a peak of 11 per cent in 1986. It then fell to around 7 per cent in 1993 before rising again to 10 per cent later in 1993. Though unemployment has since fallen to 7 per cent in November 1996 it remains stubbornly high and the general view is that the NAIRU has risen since the 1970s (this is shown by the data in Table 4.2).

Various reasons have been suggested for the rise including the effect of more generous welfare packages and the effect of new technology. Another possibility, however, is that the concentration on inflation as a target variable of economic policy has reduced aggregate demand and led to permanent increases in unemployment. The reason is that orders once lost are hard to regain, factories closed down are not easily reopened while workers who are unemployed for long periods may gradually lose hope and become unemployable. Finally, business optimism may be damaged beyond repair. Such *hysterisis* effects may well have occured in the UK and elsewhere. They suggest that it may be dangerous to rely on the simple cures for inflation suggested by the monetarists and new classical school. They also suggest that the goal of reducing inflation can be pursued with excessive zeal. Given the data of the table, readers might conclude that with such a range of estimates the concept of the NAIRU is rather too nebulous to act as a guide for policy.

Table 4.2 NAIRU estimates for the UK (percentage of workforce)

	1966–73	1974–80	1981–87	1989–90
NAIRU range	1.6–5.6	4.5–7.3	5.2–9.9	3.5–8.1
Actual unemployment rate	2.5	3.8	10.1	6.8
Number of estimates	11	13	15	5

Source: *Bank of England Quarterly Bulletin*, May 1993, p. 174

Questions

1. (a) Given that the money supply is growing by 8 per cent per annum and productivity growth is zero what would monetarists predict the rate of inflation to be?

   (b) If productivity growth rises to 3 per cent per year, what would the inflation rate now be expected to be?

   (c) Assume for some reason that output grows by 6 per cent per annum and productivity by 3 per cent per annum, what would you expect inflation to be?

   (d) How could a situation arise where inflation was zero, money supply growth was zero and output was growing by 2 per cent per annum?

2. Given the following equation:

$$p = 0.001[Y - Y_0] + 0.9[p^e] + 0.2[p^* - s]$$

and

$$Y - Y_0 = 20, \ p^e = 0.04, \ [p^* - s] = 0.06$$

what would be the inflation rate?

3. 'There is no painless cure for inflation'. Discuss.

4. Using the AD-AS model, explain how an increase in government spending financed by an expansion of the money supply will increase the rate of inflation. Will it affect output in the long-run?

5. What is natural about the 'natural rate of output'?

6. What is the NAIRU? Can it be changed by government policy?

Risk and its impact on business

> I claim not to have controlled events but confess plainly that events have controlled me. (Abraham Lincoln)

5.1 THE BUSINESS CYCLE

General trading conditions can have an important effect on the viability of individual enterprises as the events of 1979–81 and 1989–91 have dramatically shown in the UK. Such trading conditions are indicated by the business or trade cycle which typically charts the movement of real output around its trend value. Given the extent of interdependency in world markets, the business cycle usually affects all market-based industrial countries more or less simultaneously and indeed many less industrialized ones too. Nevertheless, there can be differences in the impact scale and precise timing of the cycle in particular economies reflecting a range of specific domestic influences. Figure 5.1 which gives details of the business cycle for the seven major OECD (Organization for Economic Co-operation and Development) economies demonstrates these points. Notice, for example, how the oil crisis of the early 1970s caused a major dip in GDP (gross domestic product) in all seven. Notice also how the austere monetary policies of Mrs Thatcher's UK government caused a dramatic fall in UK industrial production relative to trend in 1980.

As can also be seen from Figure 5.1 all the seven countries have clearly suffered from short-run cycles lasting from four to eight years in length, a situation which seems to be endemic to industrial societies.

In the UK, an aggregate measure of the trade cycle is used, the so-called 'coincident' indicator, and this is based on the movement of six variables. These are the three alternative estimates of GDP (income, output and expenditure), the index of manufacturing production, the index of volume of retail sales and CBI (Confederation of British Industry) industrial trends survey information on changes in stocks of materials used in production and on the number of firms working at below capacity.

Throughout the nineteenth century and up to the Second World War fluctuations in economic activity were dramatic involving from time to time significant falls in output. In the UK, for example, downturns occurred in 1907–9, 1921–4, 1926–7 and, of course, in the Great Depression after 1929. The period from the end of the war to the early 1970s was, however, unique in

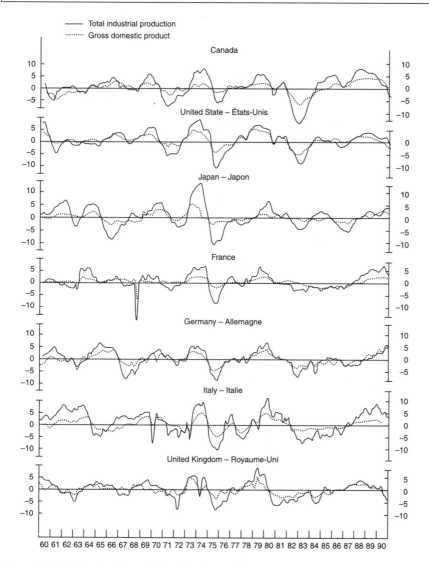

Figure 5.1 Cycles in industrial production and gross domestic product
Source: Organization for Economic Co-operation and Development (1991) *Historical Statistics*

that, during that time, recession meant a fall in the growth of output as opposed to a fall in absolute real value. Since 1974, the pre-war pattern has been re-established involving falling output and, as in the mid-1980s and early 1990s, significant increases in unemployment.

Figure 5.2 details the UK business cycle since 1976 and if we examine the 'coincident' indicator it can be seen that the country has experienced minor cycles of between four and five years in length. What is clear, however, is that the deviation from trend has recently been increasing and this explains the revival of interest in long swings. To some the deviation from trend is explained by the fact that long swings are superimposed on the short ones.

Box 5.1 Measures of the UK trade cycle

The main indicator of the UK trade cycle is the **coincident indicator**. This is a composite measure based upon GDP, output of the production industries, the CBI Quarterly Survey of below capacity utilization, the index of the volume of retail sales and the CBI quarterly survey of the percentage balance of changes in stocks of raw materials. As can be seen from Figure 5.2 the indicator was rising relative to trend since mid-1992 but may now be falling. Of course the coincident indicator describes the trend but businesses really require advance notice of future turning-points so that they can prepare for them. Some help may be provided by leading indicators of which two are shown in the figure.

The **shorter leading indicator** is based upon changes in consumer borrowing, real gross trading profits of companies, new car registrations, the CBI quarterly survey of changes in new orders (percentage balance) and expected changes in stocks of materials (percentage balance). The median lead time of this indicator relative to the coincident one is four months though this varies considerably from four to sixteen.

The **longer leading indicator** is based upon the real financial surplus or deficit of industrial and commercial companies, the CBI quarterly survey of business optimism (percentage balance), the FT 500 Share index, the rate of interest on three month prime, bank bills and total dwellings started. The median lead in this case is twelve months but it can vary from three to thirty-nine!

Very often some businesses and agencies require 'leading' information on a less aggregative basis, e.g. for particular regions or sub-regions which may be affected by the trade cycle after a lag relative to the UK as a whole. House prices, for example, tend to fall first in London and the South-East subsequently followed in order by those in the South-West, Midlands, Wales, the North and finally Scotland.

Unfortunately, much less information is available at regional level and, what there is is often out of date by the time it is received. Moreover, that on unemployment, for example, lags rather than leads the main cycle.

The Plymouth Business School *Insight* Business Activity Index (Plymouth Business School, 1996) tries to get around this problem for South-West England. The index is based upon a number of variables for some of which there are data in the public domain, e.g. new housing starts, new car registrations, mortgage possessions, job vacancies and the number unemployed, and for some of which there are not. The latter include property advertised in the local press, land charge searches, new gas connections to new housing, electricity and water consumption, various indicators of new telecommunications linkages and cessations, debit balances and number of loans made by industrial sector and jobs advertised in the local press. These data are provided by local businesses, representatives of which meet to discuss the latest trends prior to the quarterly publication of the index.

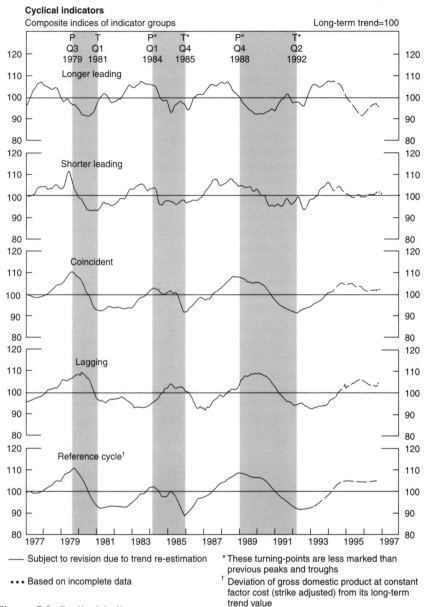

Figure 5.2 Cyclical indicators
Source: Central Statistical Office (1997)

However, there are few observations of a fifty-year cycle and so far no accepted theoretical explanation for its existence. If an explanation for the long cycle does exist, it may lie with exogenous factors such as population changes, the accumulation of new inventions, the opening up of new territories and changing patterns of trade between developed and undeveloped countries (Rostow, 1978). If these factors are crucial then the existence of long waves of similar duration may be largely coincidental and certainly many economists are sceptical about them. Either way there is no doubt about the existence of short cycles, and what these demonstrate is the risk and uncertainty involved in business. A new investment, for example, may succeed or fail depending on whether it is launched at the start of an upturn or a downturn in the cycle. Timing can be everything.

Questions

1. What do you understand by the term 'business cycle'? To what extent is it affected in any one country by:
   (a) national government policy?
   (b) international influences?
2. 'It could be argued that macroeconomic events have more effect on a business than the quality of management.' Discuss.
3. Distinguish between the terms 'long wave' and 'short wave' when discussing economic cycles.
4. How are business cycles measured in the UK?
5. What has happened to the amplitude and duration of UK cycles in output since 1960? (Use data on GDP from *Economic Trends* Annual Supplement).
6. What was different about UK economic cycles from 1945 to 1970?
7. 'The economic cycle is an international phenomenon about which governments can do nothing.' Discuss.

5.2 RISK AND THE INDIVIDUAL BUSINESS

The problem may perhaps be emphasized by showing the real difficulties involved in investment appraisal as opposed to the neat solutions suggested by the financial textbooks. Assume, for example, that the firm uses the net present value (NPV) method of appraisal and that it is considering investing in new plant to produce its product, steel ingots. The formula for the NPV is as follows:

$$NPV = A_0 + \frac{A_1}{(1 + r)^1} + \frac{A_2}{(1 + r)^2} + ... \frac{A_n}{(1 + r)^n}$$

Where A_0 is the initial capital outlay; A_1 to A_n are the net returns to the project in years 1 to n (i.e. receipts less running costs and any additional capital costs); r is the rate of interest.

In practice the solution to the problem is far from simple. What the returns will be in various years is hard to predict. Quite apart from such factors as what domestic competitor firms are doing it will depend on such influences as the level of aggregate demand in the economy and the demand for steel in particular, and this in turn is likely to be influenced by such factors as prices and exchange rates. These will be influenced by the macroeconomic policies

Table 5.1 NPV given various assumptions

	States of the world	Interest rate	
		10% *(0.6)*	*13%* *(0.4)*
Growth of GDP	3%(0.5)	£10,000	£4,000
	−1%(0.5)	−£1,000	−£4,000

of governments around the world and by the supply-side characteristics and performance of a large number of countries. Moreover, inflation will influence nominal cash receipts. But the problem does not finish here. If firms choose to borrow funds as the project unfolds, there is the additional problem of which interest rate to use as a discount factor. Rates of interest change significantly over the life of projects so this is far from an easy problem to solve. In any event, it is compounded by the existence of inflation, expectations of which will be incorporated in nominal interest rates.

The standard way to allow for such influences is to consider a range of outcomes based upon different assumptions. Meaningful figures in terms of expected outcomes can only be calculated, however, if probabilities can be attached to alternative outcomes. A simple analysis is shown in Table. 5.1.

If the probabilities are as shown in parentheses then the expected outcome is:

$$(10,000 \times 0.6 \times 0.5) + (4,000 \times 0.4 \times 0.5) + (- 1,000 \times 0.6 \times 0.5)$$
$$+ (- 4,000 \times 0.4 \times 0.5) = £2,700$$

There is an expected profit of £2,700 in the case shown in Table 3.1. In practice, however, there are many influences and many outcomes while insurance-type situations where the risks are known or can be calculated are rare. The entrepreneur, therefore, must subjectively decide if and when to invest, and in what way, given the best information of likely future events he can obtain.

5.3 ENVIRONMENTAL INFLUENCES

It will be obvious, of course, that many of the environmental influences affecting the above investment decision also affect other aspects of decision-taking in the individual enterprise. Clearly, the importance of these influences to a particular firm will depend upon the nature of its business and they may differ in importance at different points in time. What influences, then, can be identified?

The economic environment

This is clearly of great importance and is the primary concern of this book. Of significance are such factors as the level of world and domestic trade as evidenced by the trade cycle. Also of concern are the exchange rate, which will clearly affect the competitiveness of exports, imports and the price of imported raw materials, the level of interest rates and the availability of credit.

The Government

Political decisions are, of course, related to the economic environment since much of policy is economic in direction. Thus, the decision in the UK to adopt monetarist principles in the late 1970s did much to raise interest rates and influence the movement of the sterling exchange rate. This made British manufacturing industry uncompetitive in the early 1980s but strengthened the role of the City of London.

However, there are a great many other policy decisions which have an impact on business. The Government, for example, often adopts a regulatory role in setting safety standards, maximum hours of work, minimum wage levels, quality specifications, granting of patents and so on, all of which may have specific effects on particular areas of business. In some cases, these are supplemented by international law or, in the case of Europe, by the European Union.

Moreover, government decisions on pay in the public sector also affect business for comparability reasons. Similarly, the financing of pay deals in the public sector and of public expenditure generally affects levels of business taxation and, therefore, profitability. The latter may also be affected if the Government competes with the private sector for the best employees or for investment funds.

A further important government influence is through the purchase of the output of the private sector. Particular firms are greatly affected by whether they are successful in obtaining the often huge government contracts and by the systems of contracting adopted. Defence in particular is one area where specific companies have benefited from large orders and the technical expertise involved in fulfilling them. Many are now struggling following the major reductions in defence expenditure associated with the ending of the cold war.

Other political influences concern both industrial and employment policy and these may have a differential effect on different firms and/or different industrial areas.

Capital markets

We have already mentioned the importance of interest rates and will be returning to this in due course. Also of importance, however, are the attitudes of financial institutions to different types of business. It is often argued that it is more difficult to obtain venture capital in the UK than in other developed countries, particularly for small firms, and that as a result many British inventions are developed abroad. It is also argued that UK financial institutions have much more of an 'arm's length' approach to industry than is the case, for example, in West Germany where lending banks often hold large equity shareholdings in industrial companies and exercise voting rights. All this may affect the types of business which can attract funds and, therefore, the direction of economic development.

The labour market

It has already been argued that the recruitment policies of the Government and its negotiations on levels of pay will have clear spill-over effects on the private sector. Similarly, decisions in one part of the private sector will have repercussions in another, for in many cases industries and the firms which comprise them are essentially competing for the same labour force. Recent years have hardly been categorized by general labour shortages but at other times these have been important constraints on the level of output growth. Even when there is no general shortage there may still be shortages of particular types of labour such as electronics engineers which could be a severe constraint on the growth of high-technology industries. The problem is that the better qualified labour is required to be, the more difficult it is to redress labour shortages, for it takes a great deal of education and educational planning to increase the output of electronics engineers or biotechnologists. In some cases, it is necessary to change the attitudes of prospective employees and educational institutions in favour of subjects which may not traditionally have been taught or chosen to a sufficient extent. A further problem is that given the pace of technical change a particular educational investment may turn out to be obsolete even before it is completed.

Cultural and social attitudes will, of course, also be important in conditioning the supply of entrepreneurs on the one hand and labour relations on the other, both of which will be important influences on the level and type of business activity. Finally, cultural attitudes, educational standards and levels of remuneration in other countries will all affect the labour market in any one country such as the UK.

The level of technology

The events of the last two hundred years in the UK are ample evidence of the importance of technological developments in business life. In the early years of industrialization, it was inventions in the textile and iron industries which gave a major boost to the UK economy. With the ending of the age of steam, however, and the introduction of oil-based technology much of British industrial production became inefficient and/or obsolete. The process has continued in recent years where industries based on electronics have been a major feature of growth in countries such as Japan. Japanese electronics companies are now major investors in the UK and other developed countries. A further effect of technological development is that, together with improvements in communications and budgetary control techniques, it has enabled firms to differentiate their production activities from their head office functions. Little wonder then that much of production has been decentralized to low-wage regions and low-wage countries and only head offices have been retained in cities such as London, New York and Paris.

Suppliers

At the macro scale firms dependent on raw material imports will clearly be adversely affected by a depreciating exchange rate. The latter might reflect decisions in a particular important economy such as the USA or decisions by a body such as OPEC (Organization of Petroleum Exporting Countries) to raise the price of oil. Equally, movements in the exchange rate could reflect the economic performance of particular countries or the over-exploitation of particular sources of supply.

Indeed, supplies are of crucial importance to any firm, particularly if the number of alternative sources is limited. Linkages between firms in a modern economy are so complex that a strike in one supplier may directly and indirectly affect a large number of businesses. There are many examples of businesses being forced to close by events with which they were not directly involved.

Customers

Moving to the demand side, it is, of course, crucial that firms understand their market and changes in the market environment. One aspect of this is that firms or potential entrepreneurs must be aware of gaps in the market which exist or can be created and must seek to fill them. Another aspect is that firms must monitor the demand for existing products and methods of producing them so that they can remain competitive. This brings us then to a further important influence, that of competitors.

Competitors

In this respect, the firm in a particular market will be affected by the decisions of existing firms in the same market and by the potential entry of others. As far as existing competitors are concerned there will be a need to monitor all operations including price, marketing, cost, methods of production, relationships with suppliers, vertical and horizontal integration and so on. For potential entrants monitoring may be more difficult. The existing firm will need to be aware of any entry barriers which exist in the industry such as economies of scale, consumer goodwill and legal protection and of any threats of those barriers. In the case of legal protection this may come from changes in policy so that lobbying of government may be important. On the technical side, it is a case of being aware of new developments which may threaten existing markets. This may concern new production methods favouring either larger or smaller firms in the same industry or, indeed, developments in other industries which may make firms in those industries potential competitors in one's own. Thus, for example, the development of UPVC made producers of plastics competitors in the building supplies industry.

Socio-cultural influences

It has been argued (Weiner, 1981) that cultural attitudes may have been important in the relative economic decline of the UK and they have been suggested as important in the modern growth of Japan. As far as differences between countries are concerned these may affect the decisions of, for example, multinational companies as to where they site plants and this may have implications for economic development and prosperity. As for individual countries we have already argued that socio-cultural attitudes will affect risk-taking and entrepreneurship and it is this which Thatcherism attempted to improve in the UK. At the general level attitudes are certainly slow to change but change they do and firms have to be aware of this. An example is provided by the Campaign for Real Ale which curtailed the plans of the big UK brewers to move towards exclusively mass-produced keg beer.

5.4 THE CHANGING ENVIRONMENT

There are then a number of environmental influences and though they have been itemized separately they are, of course, interrelated. Many government decisions, for example, are a response to changes in the economic and socio-cultural environment. As far as the economic environment is concerned, many governments reacted to inflation by adopting monetarist policies. In the past, some have adopted protectionism in the face of economic recession. As for the socio-cultural environment, government must react to changing public attitudes. A case in point is smoking which has become increasingly prohibited as it has become increasingly socially unacceptable, and this has affected the tobacco industry and necessitated structural adjustment in places such as Bristol and Nottingham in which it was once an important industry.

But firms too are forced to adapt directly to changes in social attitudes. An example is provided by the impact of European Union (EU) legislation concerning the constituents of food products, which has increasingly drawn public attention to the use of additives. Concern that some of these additives may be toxic has affected demand and many manufacturers have now cut down on the use of these and/or swapped non-harmful for harmful ones.

Indeed, the problem for business is that all of the above environmental influences not only interact but change frequently and sometimes significantly. Manufacturing firms in the UK have, for example, been dramatically affected by the effect of North Sea oil on the exchange rate, the entry of the UK into the EU, the adoption by the Government of monetarist principles and, more recently, entry and exit from the exchange rate mechanism (ERM). They have also been affected by, and have themselves conditioned, economic policy decisions.

Similarly, firms in all developed countries have been, and are being, affected by the increased use of microelectronics and information technology. There are, of course, many other examples of environmental change such as greater concern for green issues and they all have an impact on business. The question is how to deal with it.

5.5 STRATEGY FOR RISK

There are essentially two schools of thought in terms of business strategy. The mainstream view is that the best approach is to work out coherent strategic plans encompassing a set of company objectives and a method of achieving them over the short, medium and long-term. We may call this the management science approach, on which there is a voluminous literature (e.g. Johnson and Scholes, 1990). Thus company A may say that it wishes to be a market leader in a particular product with a turnover of so many billions of pounds by the end of the next decade. University B may say that it wishes to be a major research and teaching organization by the same date. However, the problem with all such plans is that the goalposts have usually shifted by the target date so that the measures and systems used to implement the plans have become obsolete. Perhaps that is why so much of the business policy literature relies on case studies. Unfortunately, it is rarely possible to generalize from them for the world is so uncertain that today's successful Freddie Laker, John Aspinall, Robert Maxwell or Alan Bond can easily become tomorrow's business failure. What worked in the past in a particular set of circumstances may not work in the future. Of course some strategic planning may pay off, particularly over the short to medium term. It might be sensible, for example, for the firm to secure supplies and markets either through long-term purchasing agreements or by vertical integration. Similarly, the firm can attempt to ensure a market by creating conditions in which it is difficult for new firms to enter its industry. These include advertising, the use of brand names, the utilization of economies of scale and the creation of absolute cost advantages. However, such benefits may only be temporary particularly in industries where there is a fast rate of technical change. IBM, for example, invested too heavily in mainframe computers and lost a large part of its market share in computers to micros. In general, it may be argued that the days of long-term strategic plans are over and so are those of the big management teams used to plan and attempt to realize the objectives associated with them.

This leads us to the second approach to business strategy which is that the business environment is best described as a 'chaotic' system in the mathematical sense of the world. Such systems are characterized by highly complex interrelationships incorporating non-linear feedbacks which are impossible to model. As Parker and Stacey (1994) argue, the links between causes and effects are blurred and cannot be captured by simple linear systems. The behaviour of chaotic systems is highly dependent on initial conditions with small specification errors resulting in major prediction errors. Hence the often quoted case of a butterfly flapping its wings in Tokyo setting up a climatic disturbance ending up with a hurricane in New York. We might observe the hurricane but would be most unlikely to be able to trace the cause. As Parker and Stacey (1994, p. 174) continue: 'we have to understand behaviour in systematic, holistic terms rather than reductionist, casual ones'.

What this means is that the long-term future is unknowable so that the most sensible strategy is to maximize the adaptiveness of organizations to whatever comes their way. It suggests lean, responsive companies with small management teams thriving upon the opportunities continually being thrown up by the uncertainties of the business environment.

Much quoted management gurus Tom Peters (1987) and Michael Porter (1990) have gone some way down this road though both of these and John Kay (1993) still seem to think that key capabilities can be learned from previous successful business experience to form a checklist for managers in achieving long-term objectives. This, according to Parker and Stacey (1994), is arguable. Either way, at the more basic level, sensible measures to deal with uncertainty include franchising and subcontracting which, of course, largely involve shifting the risk on to someone else. Also important is diversification and this is true in a number of areas. Farmers do not wish to be dependent on individual crops, the return on which may rely on such diverse influences as the vagaries of the weather or political infighting in the EU. Similarly, it has been argued that firms in science-based industries with fast rates of technical change have to be very large so that successes can offset the inevitable failures (Pratten, 1986). The predominance of industrial conglomerates is evidence of the philosophy of 'don't keep all your eggs in one basket'.

All this suggests the demise of strategic plans and that other curse of recent times, the mission statement. It does not, however, rule out scenario-planning as practised by companies like Shell (Beck, 1981). This involves mapping out a variety of possible future scenarios relating to supplies, production, consumption and so on, considering their implications for business profitability and survival, and practising possible responses. As Parker and Stacey (1994, p. 15) point out this is not really planning at all but rather 'a form of learning intended to improve skills at responding to events as they occur'.

An economic strategy

A good deal of the uncertainty referred to in the last section is macroeconomic so it is important to consider how businesses can deal with macroeconomic risk. For those who believe in linear predictable outcomes, the management scientists as we have called them, there is the possibility of using leading indicators and economic forecasts. Both are essentially dependent on the viewpoint that what has happened in the past is likely to happen in the future. This is more likely to be true over the short-run than the long-run if it is true at all.

The simplest approach is to make use of leading indicators two of which are shown in Figure 5.2. Leading indicators are those which precede and signal changes in the economy generally. Thus, in the UK, a longer leading indicator is composed of the *Financial Times* (FT) share index and evidence on housing starts and business confidence. A shorter leading indicator is based on such evidence as new car registrations, company profits and changes in industrial demand (see Box 5.1). However, as will be obvious, these factors will already be influencing and influenced by a large number of businesses before they are published and, therefore, their usefulness is limited. A further difficulty is that the reliability of the leading indicators may change as the components on which they are based change in importance. Thus tax changes on company cars may make new car registrations a less reliable measure than hitherto while the changing perception of housing as an investment may have the same impact on housing starts. One way around the problem is for business persons to extrapolate trends but, since the cycle is of irregular length, this is unlikely to be practicable.

What then of economic forecasts? Extensive use is made of these by numerous businesses, government departments, local authorities and quangos over the short, medium and long-term but, as we shall see in the next chapter, they should be used with care. One reason, of course, is that economists have a very imprecise knowledge of how the economy works despite enormous investments in multi-equation econometric models. This brings us back to chaos theory, for if it applies to the world economy it is hardly surprising that even complex linear equation systems are unable to predict accurately. This squares with the more limited criticism of Lucas (1976) that the parameters of macroeconometric models are unlikely to be stable in response to fundamental changes in policy affecting the behaviour of individuals.

This brings us to alternative approaches among which economic-scenario planning may well be of some use. So may be taking advantage of those opportunities which do exist to avoid or reduce uncertainty. One such measure is the use of forward markets. These set a price 'today' for future delivery of goods (e.g. wheat) or financial assets (e.g. foreign exchange) and allow firms to hedge against future changes in 'spot' prices. Speculators often adopt a middle role and by matching buyers and sellers usually ensure that forward markets work efficiently. Given the increasing internationalization of production and financial markets, it is hardly surprising that forward markets are very important features of dealing in both money and commodities.

A third possibility is the use of a portfolio of assets, both financial and tangible. In this respect, firms may be compared with individuals in that they spread risks by having a portfolio of industrial shares and other financial assets. Some of these may be high risk in that they rise or fall faster than the stock market index, some are low risk in that they tend to rise or fall slower than the market and some move in the opposite direction to the market. Increasingly, assets are held internationally, which is a further method of reducing risk. One aspect of this portfolio diversification is that firms may undertake production in a number of countries, thus switching production between various plants depending on local cost conditions. Good examples here are multinational car firms, where different parts of the same car can be made in different countries.

It is these elements of planning and minimizing risk from changes in the macroeconomy which form the major part of this book and we now examine them in some detail. We begin with a look at economic forecasting.

Questions

1. To what extent does the business cycle impinge upon business decisions?
2. How can firms deal with risk caused by changes in macroeconomic events?
3. Explain the following terms 'coincident indicator', 'longer leading indicator', 'shorter leading indicator'. How are they calculated?
4. How useful are leading indicators for business planning?
5. If you were looking for leading indicators of business activity in your locality, what would you use?
6. Explain the term 'chaos theory' and consider its implications for strategic planning.
7. If chaos exists, how valid are the strategic perspectives of a) Michael Porter or b) Tom Peters.
8. 'The value of "scenario-planning" is easily over-estimated.' Discuss.

6 The use of forecasts

The purpose of economic forecasting is to make astrology look respectable.
(Ezra Solomon)

It was argued in Chapter 5 that a method of reducing risk as far as the macroeconomic environment is concerned was to use economic forecasts to anticipate the future. Such forecasts are based on models which, like the economy itself, are extremely complex. They are macroeconomic models which give a mathematical representation of the quantitative relationships between such variables as employment, output, consumption, investment, prices, interest rates and exchange rates. A large number of equations are involved including both identities reflecting the national income accounting framework and behavioural equations which describe the aggregate actions of consumers, producers, investors and so on. The numerical values of the parameters in the behavioural equations are usually determined by statistical

---

Box 6.1 UK forecasting models

There are numerous forecasting models of the UK economy including those of the Treasury, which uses its model for policy purposes, international organizations including the OECD, the International Monetary Fund (IMF), the European Union and national independent institutions such as the CBI, National Institute of Economic and Social Research (NIESR), Liverpool University, the London Business School, Cambridge Econometrics and Business Strategies Ltd. In the UK, outside agencies are allowed to run forecasts on the Treasury model and the ITEM club representing a group of academics and businessmen is one that does so. There are currently some seventeen forecasting institutions of the above categories whose forecasts are monitored by the Treasury (e.g. HM Treasury, 1996). In addition there are numerous 'City' institutions which produce forecasts on a regular basis. The forty plus currently monitored by the Treasury include those of domestic and international banks and stockbrokers such as Barclays, National Westminster, Chase Manhattan, Credit Lyonnais, J P Morgan, Goldman Sachs and S G Warburg.

Of course the models vary in sophistication ranging from tens to hundreds of equations and, as argued in the main text, they reflect the underlying theoretical beliefs of the model-builders and in some cases the data to which they have access. Many are eclectic.

estimation from historical data. Even so it would be unwise to believe that forecasting is a completely scientific exercise. On the contrary estimating exogenous variables and the adjustment of forecast output give plenty of scope for 'art'.

6.1 FORECASTING MODELS

The construction of economy-wide models has developed over the last thirty years, facilitated by data improvements and advances in econometric techniques and computer technology (Whitley, 1994). The models themselves change over time in response to such influences as developments in theory, empirical evidence, performance and institutional arrangements. Some disappear as funding from sources such as the UK Research Councils dries up.

As can be seen from the data in Table 6.1, there are considerable differences in the output of the various forecasting teams despite a general unwillingness to step out of line. This is no doubt on the grounds that it looks better to be wrong in a group than wrong individually.

Such differences occur for a number of reasons including different model structures based upon different theoretical perceptions of how economies work, because of the usage of different information, because the purpose of the model is different, because of different expectations of the movement of

Table 6.1 Economic forecasts, 1996 (percentage change on one year earlier[1])

	Average	Highest	Lowest
GDP	2.7	3.3	1.4
Consumer's expenditure	2.5	3.3	1.3
Government expenditure	1.0	2.5	0.0
Fixed investment	6.1	8.7	0.4
Stockbuilding £bn	2.0	6.5	−0.3
Domestic demand	2.6	3.4	0.9
Exports	5.6	8.1	2.2
Imports	5.3	8.1	1.6
RPI	3.1	4.3	1.4
Average earnings	4.3	5.2	3.2
Sterling index Q4	84.4	88.0	80.1
Interest rate Q4%	6.9	7.8	5.3
Oil price $	17.3	23.0	15.0
Employment	0.9	9.0	0.0
Claimant unemployed (M)	2.12	2.55	1.81
Industrial production	2.9	3.6	1.5
World trade	6.1	7.8	2.9
Current account (£bn)	−4.5	10.8	−13.0
PSBR[2] (£bn 96–97)	22.6	30.0	15.0

Note: [1] Unless defined otherwise.
[2] PSBR = public sector borrowing requirement. These figures are in £bn and relate to 1996–97
Source: HM Treasury (1995).

exogenous variables (i.e. those not estimated within the forecasting model) and because of different applications of 'tender loving care'. This involves considerable work in adjusting the raw output of the model to take account of special influences and perhaps more cynically to obtain desired results.

To demonstrate some of these points, consider the simple Keynesian text-book model of Chapter 2, a closed-economy version of which contains just one identity and one behavioural equation:

$$Y = C + G \tag{6.1}$$

$$C = a + bY + u \qquad o < b < 1 \tag{6.2}$$

where Y = output (GDP); C = consumers' expenditure; G = government expenditure and u is a zero-mean random error term. The model is solved by substituting for C in (6.1) to give the 'reduced form':

$$Y = \frac{a + G + u}{1 - b} = K(a + G + u) \tag{6.3}$$

In this case, k = 1/(1 − b) is the 'multiplier' and measures the impact on Y of a unit change in G. In this simple model, it is determined by the size of the marginal propensity to consume out of income, i.e. b. The larger b is, the larger is the multiplier.

Even in this simple case of one model, forecasts of output by two rival forecasting bodies may differ in this case because

- of different assumptions about the future course of the exogenous variable, government expenditure, G;
- a different value is assumed for the marginal propensity to consume, b (this is usually described as a difference in the structure of the model);
- different 'add factors', residual or intercept adjustments, u, are used to take account of 'special factors' expected to operate in the future or to account for the fact that recent values of u, the error term, are not random (but, for example, have all recently been positive). This is the 'tender, loving care' already referred to;
- the coefficient 'a' could represent 'other' influences on consumption such as interest rates. Forecasting teams differ over what variables to include in an equation as well as the size of their impact.

In practice, the models differ in structure for a whole variety of reasons including different theoretical foundations. Though some are based very heavily on a particular theoretical foundation most are eclectic having both Keynesian and monetarist characteristics. An exception is the Liverpool model which is firmly based on new classical, rational expectations principles. There are many to choose from. Details of a variety of UK and foreign models are given in Whitley (1994).

Many businesses subscribe to the output of at least one of the forecasting teams though why they do so is perhaps arguable given the frequent poor performance of the forecasters (see Box 6.2). Not only do forecasters tend to be inaccurate, they tend to be most inaccurate when there are turning-points in

Box 6.2 Firms and forecasts

Economic forecasting consultancy was according to Marsh (1993) a boom industry during the UK recession of the early 1990s. One reason was the perceived benefits to companies from accurate prediction of economic events. Marsh reports in this regard the case of the Prudential insurance company which converted a significant amount of its sterling holdings into other currencies ahead of the devaluation of September 1992. Another important factor in the growth of economics consultancy was that competition between consultants had driven down prices relative to the cost of employing in-house economists.

Finally, using a consultancy enables firms to 'plug in' to a network of other businesses which use the same consultancy. They, therefore, benefit potentially from seminars and other meetings which discuss economic prospects. As can be seen from Table 6.2, the potential for this type of networking is large.

Table 6.2 Some UK consultants and clients, 1993

Consultant	Turnover £	Staff No.	Clients No.	Examples
Business Strategies	800,000	15	50	Blue Circle, BASF, BT
Cambridge Econometrics	1 m	19	50	IBM, water companies, TECs
Centre for Economics and Business Research	n.a.	4	24	3I, Siemens, IBM
DRI	40 m	450	600	CM, Chevron BP
Item Club	150,000	2	22	Bass, BAe, Midland
Henley Centre	5 m	70	n.a.	BT, Glaxo
London Business School	n.a.	27	16	IBM, Barclays, Unilever, Shell
Oxford Economic Forecasting	1 m	20	100	ICI, Digital, GKN, BP
WEFA	30 m	275	4000	Unilever, RTZ, Barclays

Source: Marsh (1993)

As can be seen, some companies use more than one consultant, a wise approach given that the forecasters so often get things wrong. Perhaps, what is really surprising is that such extensive use is made of forecasters in view of this point. Marsh quotes Doug McWilliams, head of the Centre for Economics and Business Research at that time, who argued that 'in the kingdom of the blind, the one-eyed man is king'. The argument, therefore, seems to be that economic forecasters are likely to be less wrong than others in a world of great uncertainty and that their advice may turn out to be beneficial. Doubtless, there are times when this is true and times when it is more arguable. For a cynical view of economic forecasting see Peck (1993).

the economic cycle, probably the very time when they are most needed. Ironically, despite the fact that few of the major forecasting teams predicted the onset or depth of the 1989–92 recession, the purchase of economic forecasts by business was one of the few recession-proof industries (Marsh, 1993).

Businesses use such forecasts in a variety of ways. The simplest approach is to take the output of a major forecasting team such as the London Business School and utilize the results in planning output levels, new product launches and so on. The problem with this approach is that the output of such models is rarely specific to the output of the business in question. There may, for example, be a prediction for consumption or even consumable durables but there may be a big difference between the prospects of consumer durables in general and specific 'white goods' such as refrigerators. One approach is to buy in or develop a 'satellite' model in which the output of interest to the firm, refrigerators, is linked to that of the white goods forecast by the aggregate model. Many companies have adopted this approach (Marsh, 1993). Other examples of satellite models are regional and sub-regional models driven largely by the output of the national model. In this case, the output of the national model is distributed around the regions.

Of course, most businesses are aware of the fallibility of the forecasters and should sensibly use forecast output to develop one of a range of alternative scenarios on which not too much reliance should be put. They can, moreover, increasingly 'tweak' the output of the models the latest versions of which can be purchased for use on personal computers. Thus the business person can put in alternative estimates of exogenous variables to work out a range of estimates of model output. Such simulations can provide a number of potential possible scenarios and the sensitivity of the business to them may be assessed. By way of an example, suppose a businesswoman feels that the publicly available forecasts are too pessimistic on the outlook for world trade since she has 'inside' marketing information from her sales force and overseas subsidiaries. All she has to do is to put in her set of figures for world trade and the model will produce (usually graphically) the difference between the central forecast and the businesswoman's 'new' forecast. The advantage in using the computer model is that it is likely to embody all the main 'feedbacks' in the economy. For example, higher world trade directly boosts exports but may lead to an appreciation in the exchange rate and some loss in price competitiveness which will attenuate export growth. The impact of export growth in the domestic market (via the multiplier) and on domestic prices will also be printed out by the model's solution programme. Hence the businesswoman can assess the impact of her alternative assumptions about overseas demand on domestic demand, domestic cost and price inflation. If she is willing to repeat the exercise for alternative scenarios then she can apply the rules of decision-making under uncertainty (e.g. maximin, expected values) to rank her options (see Lumby, 1984).

Ideally one would like to assess the sensitivity of a central forecast to changes in the parameters (e.g. the marginal propensity to consume, 'b' of the model above) as well as to changes in exogenous variables (e.g. world trade or government expenditure, G). The former capability is not yet widely available.

However the business uses forecast output, it must first decide on which output to choose an issue to which we now turn.

6.2 CHOOSING A FORECAST

A flavour of what is involved may be gained by looking at a range of sample forecasts as depicted in Table 6.1. These refer to the year 1996 and were made at various times during the previous year. They only relate to some of the variables included in the forecasts and even here comparison is complicated by differences in variable definition and inclusion and, occasionally, by slight differences in the time period to which the forecasts on individual variables relate. There are substantial differences between the forty or so forecasts on which the table is based. How then can the business interpret this bewildering amount of information.

One alternative would be to use the forecasts of those forecasting bodies which have done well or more cynically *relatively* well in the past. An example of simple ranking procedures is the annual assessment of the *Independent* newspaper. This involves the construction of a 'guru' index based upon the absolute difference between forecast and outturn added over three variables – price rises, unemployment and growth of GDP (see Box 6.3). A problem with this approach is that subsequent data revisions may mean that the forecaster who seemed at first to do well and get the appropriate plaudits may subsequently turn out to have been off course. More generally, ranking forecasts turns out to be far more difficult than it might appear. This is easily demonstrated with ranking forecasts for an earlier year by comparing the forecast output with what actually happened. This is done for 1990 as shown in Table 6.4. Table 6.5 summarizes the performance of the three major forecasts listed. What is clear is that there is no forecast which performs best for all variables. Indeed, the top and bottom prizes seem to be well shared out.

This is clearly a snapshot of a few variables at a point in time and what is really required is a detailed analysis of forecast performance relative to many variables over a long time period. Most forecasters do in fact assess the performance of their own forecasts and some, including the NIESRs, compare some of the major ones.

A start on long-period assessment has been made by the macroeconomics modelling bureau of the University of Warwick. This produces an annual assessment of models (e.g. Wallis *et al.*, 1987 and the subsequent articles in the *National Institute Economic Review*, e.g. Church *et al.*, 1995). There are clear difficulties given, of course, definitional differences, and the large number of variables involved. A major additional factor is that the models from which the forecasts are developed are themselves adapted over time as the forecasters try to improve their performance (Wallis *et al.*, 1987; Keating, 1985).

It is these types of difficulty which also confront the business in trying to rank the forecasts. Our assessment is that while some forecasters possibly do

Box 6.3 Golden guru awards

The *Independent* newspaper publishes an annual assessment of economic forecasts based upon the absolute value in percentage points of the difference between the actual and forecast values for just three variables (e.g. Coyle, 1996). These are GDP growth, inflation and unemployment. Table 6.3 gives the results for 1995, listing the three best and worst forecasts out of 42 examined. All the forecasts were made between November 1994 and January 1995.

Table 6.3 Economic forecasts for 1995

	GDP %	Inflation %	Unemployment %	Absolute error % Points
Top 3				
NIESR	2.7	2.8	7.9	0.37
Lehman Brothers	2.8	2.8	8.1	0.38
London Business School	2.7	3.1	8.3	0.56
Bottom 3				
S G Warburg	4.5	2.8	7.2	2.89
UBS	4.3	3.3	7.2	2.99
Société Generale	4.2	4.2	7.2	3.79
Average Forecast	3.2	2.8	8.0	0.78
Actual	2.6	2.9	8.0	n.a.

Source: Coyle (1996)

Of course, subsequent revisions to data could change these rankings which might in any case be different if other variables were looked at.

As can be seen the average seems to perform quite well, which begs the question as to why individual forecasters are prepared to 'stick their neck out' and depart from the consensus. The answer seems to lie in commercial considerations, for offering a forecast that is distinctive seems the only way an economist can build a distinctive reputation and gain new clients. If they turn out to be right, they will get press attention, new clients and monetary rewards, while if they are wrong hopefully no one will notice. It is interesting that two of the best three performers are academic teams where, perhaps, the above commercial considerations are less pressing.

perform particularly badly for long periods, among the others different forecasters do best at different times. Finally, it clearly depends on which forecast variable we are dealing with so that there are no easy answers. We, therefore, now turn to a second possible course of action which is to use a consensus forecast for business purposes. Though there is no mathematical reason for an average of forecasts to outperform that of an individual forecasting team, there is some long-term evidence to suggest that in practice it tends to do so.

Table 6.4 Comparison of forecasts for 1990 (percentage change on previous year[1])

| Variable | Forecast and date | | | Average | Spread of forecast projections[3] | | Actual |
	Treasury March 1990	NIESR February 1990	LBS February 1990		Low	High	
1. GDP	1.00	1.40	1.00	1.30	0.60	2.70	0.50
2. Private consumption	1.25	1.70	1.10	1.30	0.40	2.10	1.00
3. Government expenditure	0.25	0.90	0.30	0.90	−1.20	3.50	1.75
4. Gross fixed investment	−1.25	−2.80	−0.10	−0.50	−10.00	3.20	1.75
5. Export	7.25	7.95	8.50	7.60	4.00	8.50	4.75
6. Imports	1.00	0.80	1.50	1.20	−1.10	3.40	1.50
7. RPI	7.25	6.80	6.80	7.10	3.80	8.00	10.00
8. Average earnings	—	9.30	8.90	9.20	7.60	9.70	9.50
9. Adult unemployment (millions)	—	1.63	1.72	1.72	1.60	1.80	1.60
10. World trade	6.00	5.30	4.70	5.70	4.60	6.90	5.00
11. PSBR[2]	−7.00	−11.90	−11.30	−8.60	−13.50	−5.90	−0.75

Notes: [1] Except unemployment; occasionally changes are for slightly different periods. It should be emphasized that there are differences in the definition of variables.
[2] PSBR = public sector borrowing requirement. These figures relate to the financial year 1990–1.
[3] These figures apply to twelve major non-city forecasts.
Source: HM Treasury (1990); Central Statistical Office (1991a).

Table 6.5 Forecast performance, 1990[1]

Variable	Best	Worst
GDP	TR/LBS	NIESR
Private consumption	LBS	NIESR
Government expenditure	NIESR	TR
Gross fixed investment	TR	LBS
Export	TR	LBS
Imports	LBS	NIESR
RPI	TR	NIESR/LBS
Average earnings	NIESR	LBS
Adult unemployment	NIESR	LBS
World trade	NIESR/LBS	TR
PSBR	TR	LBS

Note: [1] LBS = London Business School, NIESR = National Institute of Economic and Social Research, TR = HM Treasury.

Even so, the average does not rank well on the basis of the 1990 evidence from Table 6.4.

Perhaps the answer is to pick a forecast by some random manner, after all it will probably turn out to be wrong. Given our early discussion of chaos theory it should come as no surprise that, despite enormous investments producing highly complex models, economists have failed to deliver models which are consistently accurate. They are fully aware of the defects of the standard approach and have increasingly begun to explore alternative approaches. One is the use of vector autoregressive (VAR) models in which each variable is regressed on a lagged series of all the other variables in the model. There is no attempt to explain how economic variables are causally related to each other and as a result this approach is of no use for policy analysis. VAR models can, however, be used to forecast the future and do not require the estimation of exogenous variables, a major problem with the traditional econometric method.

A second approach is the use of financial spread variables to give warnings of turning-points in the economic cycle. One such spread is the ratio of bond to equity prices, a narrowing meaning that the financial markets were anticipating recession, a possibility which could be self-fulfilling. This hardly results in precise estimates of the future course of economic activity.

6.3 CONCLUSION

It is easy to be cynical about the value of economic forecasts but they have been examined in some detail here, given that so many businesses use them. Though macroeconomic forecasts can, occasionally, be useful they should be used with care. One reason is that there are periods when the forecasters, not surprisingly, get things seriously wrong. As in the world of chaos theory, small changes in the parameters may make major changes to the accuracy of forecasts as may more fundamental shifts which we know occur, for example, in the savings ratio, velocity of circulation or investment value of houses. Sometimes, as Lucas (1976) has argued, such shifts are the result of government policy changes. Lucas (1976) makes the point that if the authorities drastically alter their policy stance, then the estimated coefficients of econometric equations based on past behaviour may no longer be valid.

The particular importance of the Lucas critique depends upon the severity of regime changes and their creditability. Forecasters, by making residual adjustments, attempt to take account in an *ad hoc* way of 'minor' regime changes and announcements. In practice, the fact that many existing econometric relationships exhibit stable coefficients over time (Hendry, 1983) provides some evidence that the practical importance of the Lucas critique and possibly the implications of chaos theory outlined in Chapter 5 may be overstated. It is only, perhaps, when modelling behaviour in money, bond and foreign exchange markets that the Lucas critique needs more careful consideration.

A second reason for care is that there are many different forecasting institutions and there is no simple way of choosing between alternative models on the basis of past performance. One approach for businesses is to obtain a 'copy' of a favoured model and use their own estimates and tender loving care to produce a central forecast. Either this or the central forecast of the modelling team can then be augmented with a sensitivity analysis based on different exogenous variable paths or different add-on factors. Such simulations should be considered as no more than a guide to what may actually happen.

As far as the economic forecasters are concerned, it might be beneficial if they were more prepared to publish a range of outcomes rather than a single result for each variable, and to thereby acknowledge the art involved in the forecasting process. Unfortunately, there are too many consumers only too prepared to believe that what they are told will happen will actually happen, especially if they have paid large sums of money to be told it. As the joke goes: 'It shows economists have a sense of humour. They forecast to two decimal places.'

Questions

1. Why are there so many agencies producing forecasts of the UK economy?
2. Why do economic forecasts differ?
3. Explain the following terms: 'behavioural equation', 'structural equation', 'residual, constant', 'exogenous and endogenous variable', 'add-on factor'.
4. To what extent and in what ways might forecasts using large-scale macroenonomic models be subject to judgemental elements?
5. Should we expect economists to produce accurate forecasts?
6. Why is it so difficult to rank economic forecasts?
7. 'Forecasting is a bogus scientific exercise, the results of which, if used at all, should be used with great caution.' Discuss.
8. What are satellite economic models; how useful are they?
9. What do you understand by the term 'sensitivity analysis' in the forecasting context?
10. (a) Using data from *Economic Trends* and the *Society of Motor Manufacturers and Traders*, try and develop and defend a forecasting equation for UK sales of new cars in the 1980s.
    (b) Using data for 1990 and 1991, use your forecasting equation to predict car sales for those years.
    (c) Compare your forecasts with the actual figures; comment on and, if possible, explain the differences.
    (d) Develop a satellite model for explaining the sales of any one UK manufacturer.
    (e) Suggest ways in which the models might be improved. (Note that you will need knowledge of regression analysis and access to a computer regression package to answer this question.)
11. Consider the usefulness of VAR and financial spread models for economic and business forecasting.
12. Explain the term 'Lucas' critique. What are its implications for economic forecasting?
13. Explain the links, if any, between the Lucas critique and chaos theory.

7 Exchange rates

> It does not mean that the pound in your pocket has been devalued.
>
> (Harold Wilson)

7.1 INTRODUCTION

The international influences on business have become increasingly important over time and this process looks set to continue in the future. One important influence is improvements in communications and budgetary control techniques which have enabled manufacturing firms to differentiate their production activities from their head office functions. This has contributed to a great internationalization of production as firms have sought to take advantage of cheap sources of labour in, for example, the less developed countries.

Such internationalization of production has also occurred as firms have grown in size to become multinationals operating in many markets around the world, a process which has been fostered by the gradual abolition of tariff barriers and quotas since the 1960s. Moreover, many service firms in, for example, banking, shipping, insurance and tourism operate in international markets and many in other fields are increasingly doing so. One reason for this is the link between manufacturing and services. There are clear advantages for a major UK manufacturing multinational in having, for example, the same firm of accountants or advertising consultants in London, New York and Sydney.

The liberation of exchange controls in many countries has also been an important influence in fostering the setting up of subsidiaries overseas and in the formation of international conglomerates in general. Many UK firms such as BP and Unilever have foreign subsidiaries, and a large number of others are subsidiaries of foreign-based companies. Recent examples of foreign firms buying UK subsidiaries are the Southern Electric Company of Georgia, USA (owner of SWEB) and the Swiss firm Nestlés (owners of Rowntree).

But it is not only multinationals which have been affected by changes in the international environment. The expansion of demand in industrial countries and an increase in tourism have increased the demand for foreign goods. Thus firms such as Sainsbury in the UK now stock a far wider range of foreign drinks and foreign food than they did even a decade ago. There is as a result an increased willingness to accept 'foreign' goods and services in the UK generally, which means that even producers who buy inputs locally and sell their output in the domestic market are likely to be affected by foreign competition. Imports in the UK, for example, as a percentage of GDP (at factor cost and 1980 prices) increased from 24.4 per cent in 1970 to 32.9 per cent in 1994. Finally, it should be pointed out that not only has international trade become more important, the prices at which it has been carried out have become more volatile since the abolition of fixed exchange rates in 1972. This volatility means that large swings may occur in the value of a currency over quite short periods, swings which may not accurately reflect underlying economic conditions or fundamentals.

An example, is provided by the US dollar which 'fell' from around 1.05$/£ early in 1985 to more than 1.40$/£ later in that year. It continued to fall subsequently to an average value of 1.64 in 1987 and to a value of 1.83 in March 1988.[1] Such movements in exchange rates can have very important effects on the profitability of overseas sales and the cost of imported raw materials.

European exports of cars, to the USA in particular, were badly affected by the falling dollar (i.e. *rising* deutschmark, pound, French franc exchange rates against the dollar). The dollar prices of West European cars rose in America by over a third from 1985 to 1988 and as a result sales fell. In the first half of 1988, for example, American imports of these cars were 12 per cent lower than in the same period of 1987. Volvo, Porsche and Audi were among the hardest hit. Jaguar in the UK was also affected and partly as a result pre-tax profit fell from £121m in 1986 to £97m in 1987. More recently the withdrawal of the UK from the ERM and the subsequent fall in the value of the pound dramatically improved UK exports from 1992 (see Box 7.1).

7.2 THE IMPACT OF EXCHANGE RATES ON BUSINESS

It appears then that movements of exchange rates are of great importance. Consider, for example, the case of a UK textile manufacturing firm selling suits in America to be delivered three months from now for which a US importer agrees to pay $100 each. If, over the intervening time period, the dollar depreciates from 1.5$/£ to 1.75$/£ the UK firm will clearly make a lot less money than it thought. More generally, we may look at the case of a UK manufacturing firm which sells in the domestic and foreign market and which buys in from abroad large quantities of raw materials, capital equipment and semi finished products. Because of possible changes in exchange rates it will be difficult to forecast costs of production and the gains from holding stocks of inventories because costs in home country currency will be unpredictable. Equally on the sales side there may well be lead times between the date a contract is signed and the date of delivery when returns in foreign currency accrue. Thus if our UK firm agrees to supply goods in three months' time to a US firm with the contract fixed in dollars, it may face substantial gains or losses in pounds sterling if the dollar/sterling exchange rate changes over the interval. Alternatively if the UK firm prices its goods in sterling and sterling appreciates against the dollar, the firm may find that it loses its US sales.

Box 7.1 Exports and the exchange rate

There seems little doubt that withdrawal from the ERM significantly improved the competitiveness of British industry in world markets and contributed greatly to the fact that exports were of crucial importance in pulling the UK economy out of recession from 1992 onwards. As can be seen from Table 7.1, while sterling declined by around 12 percentage points from 1992, export volumes increased by around 20 percentage points.

Table 7.1 Sterling index and export volume

	Sterling index (1990 = 100)	Export volume (1990 = 100)
1988	105.3	89.0
1989	102.3	94.2
1990	100.0	100.0
1991	100.7	101.2
1992	96.9	103.7
1993	88.9	107.4
1994	89.2	118.6
1995	84.8	124.1

Source: Office for National Statistics (1996), pp. T22, T28

Conversely the rapid appreciation of the pound in the period 1979–81 made imports highly competitive in the domestic UK market with the result that many British firms went to the wall

Indeed, some two million manufacturing jobs were lost during the period, many as a result of the exchange rate appreciation, and they have never been regained.

Table 7.2 Sterling/dollar exchange rate and import voume

	Sterling/dollar exchange rate	Import volume (1990 = 100)
1977	1.75	51.1
1978	1.92	53.5
1979	2.12	58.6
1980	2.33	55.4
1981	2.02	53.3

Source: Office for National Statistics (1996/7), pp. 143, 224

An international firm also faces the possibility of exchange rate risk if the firm is considering investing in overseas assets. These could be foreign government bonds, shares in foreign companies or fixed assets such as land and buildings. The problem now is that investment occurs today in the currency of the country in which the assets are to be purchased, while a stream of returns will occur in the future which shareholders will require remitted in domestic currency.

Exchange risk is clearly, then, of considerable importance in modern business. How much the firm can do about it will partly depend upon its leverage over price, an issue to which we now turn.

Question

1. 'Exchange rates are very volatile.' Discuss.

Pricing and overseas sales

Homogeneous products

There are a number of well-developed, international 'spot' markets for homogeneous products such as the oil market in Rotterdam where prices are quoted in dollars. A UK firm selling in such a market has to sell at the prevailing international dollar price and in all probability can sell what it wants at that price. It, therefore, faces a horizontal demand curve or price line for its product. If so, the implications of a change in the \$/£ exchange rate are straightforward.[1]

An appreciation in sterling results in a squeeze on domestic profit margins while a depreciation has the opposite effect. Take, for example, the case of a marginal North Sea oilfield from which oil may be extracted at £8.57 per barrel. If the exchange rate is 1.75\$/£, this is a cost in dollar terms of \$15.00. If the world market price of crude oil of the same quality is \$18 a barrel then the profit margin is \$3 per barrel. In *sterling* terms this is equal to $3/1.75 = £1.71$ which yields a profit margin over sterling cost of $1.71/8.57 = 19.6$ per cent. Now if sterling appreciates to 1.95\$/£ and costs remain unchanged at £8.57 a barrel, then profit is squeezed to $18 - 6.7 = \$1.3$ a barrel. In sterling terms this means a return of just £0.66 per barrel, a rate of return on cost of only 7.8 per cent.

In practice, of course, there may be some offsetting reductions in cost if, for example, there is imported US equipment used on North Sea oil rigs or if the reduction in sterling import prices feeds through into retail prices and lower wage claims. The latter, however, might take a considerable time to work through.

What then will be the effects of these changes on UK oil firms. This is illustrated in Figure 7.1. The line D_0 shows the demand curve for a UK oil firm at a world price of \$18 and an exchange rate of 1.75\$/£ = £10.3 per barrel. The line D_1 shows the demand curve after the appreciation of sterling to 1.95 (\$/£). The sterling price is then $18/1.95 = £9.2$ per barrel. The profit-maximizing firm will produce up to the point where revenue received per barrel equals the marginal cost of producing the last barrel. Thus at price 10.3, output Q_0 is produced while at price 9.2, output is cut back to Q_1. If cost reductions then accrue because of the sterling appreciation so that the marginal cost curve shifts to the right (= MC_1), then output will rise to Q_2.

To sum up, the effect of an appreciation of sterling is a squeeze on the profit margins of those UK companies that must sell homogeneous products at the

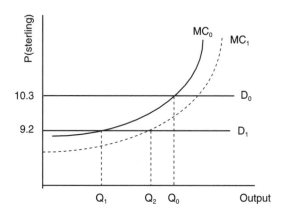

Figure 7.1 Output response of a UK oil company to a change in the exchange rate and sterling price

world market price. This in turn is likely to lead to output and employment contractions at least in the short-term.

Heterogeneous products

In practice most manufacturing (and service) firms produce output which is to some extent different from that of competitors. In such circumstances they face a downward-sloping demand curve because as prices rise, brand loyalty ensures that not all customers are lost to rival firms with lower prices. What this means in practice is that firms have some discretion over the price they charge in both domestic and international markets. In the international context, an appreciation of the home country's exchange rate means that its products and services are now less competitive in world markets. But a UK firm, for example, selling a heterogeneous product (like a Jaguar car) can trade off volume changes against price changes since it does not lose all of its market in the USA if it raises its dollar price. The point is that given the downward-sloping demand curve, it will now lose some sales but will be selling each unit at a higher dollar price. Indeed total sterling revenue might decrease very little if foreign demand is sufficiently price inelastic.

Suppose, for example, a UK firm is selling a sophisticated machine tool priced at £20,000 and at an exchange rate of 1.75$/£, this means a US price of $35,000. Let us assume it sells 100 at this price in the US. If sterling now appreciates to 1.95$/£, the UK manufacturer has two choices. The firm could still sell at the old dollar price of $35,000 which will return only £17,949 per unit in home currency and clearly involves a significantly reduced profit margin. Alternatively it could decide to raise the US price to, say, $37,500 in the hope that it will not lose all its sales at this price. Assume sales fall to ninety-five then total dollar returns are $3,562,500 which in UK currency is £1,826,923. This compares with an original sterling return of £2,000,000 before the exchange rate change and one of £1,794,900 if option one had been taken. Clearly, in this case option two is the sensible one but if sales had been eighty-five instead of ninety-five the opposite would have been true. In general the more specialized the product and the greater the buoyancy in world markets, the greater the increase in the dollar price the UK firm may be able to extract without causing a major loss of orders.

The firm's decision will also be affected by cost considerations. If, for example, the firm is operating under economies of scale (i.e. unit costs fall as output expands) the reduction in output caused by raising US prices will increase unit costs and reduce profit. The pricing decision described above is depicted in Figure 7.2. Demand curve D_0 shows sales in the US for a variety of UK sterling prices at an exchange rate of 1.75. There is an associated marginal revenue curve, MR_0, and a marginal cost curve, MC, which in this case is drawn as upward-sloping. The firm maximizes profit by selling Q_0 at price P_0. If the exchange rate rises to 1.95, sales fall at any previous sterling price so we have new demand and MR curves, D_1 and MR_1. The profit-maximizing sterling price which the firm may not know is now P_1 and the output Q_1.[2]

It should perhaps be pointed out, however, that in practice there may be no reaction to an exchange rate change in the short-run. Changing prices is costly and will have ramifications on dealers, agents, output, employment and 'goodwill' so firms may wait and see whether exchange rate changes are permanent or transitory before deciding on any actions. What a firm eventually does in response to changes in exchange rates may also depend upon its circumstances. Thus if a UK firm has recently suffered a severe profits squeeze in either home or overseas market it may (assuming inelastic demand) respond to an appreciation of sterling by raising dollar prices considerably. Conversely a firm with a strong profits position could use the opportunity of a depreciation in exchange rates to look for overseas volume turnover by keeping prices and profit margins low. It may be particularly interested in this sort of policy if stocks of unsold 'finished' goods are high.

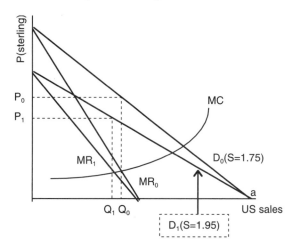

Figure 7.2 Effect of an appreciation of the $/£ exchange rate on a UK firm with a heterogeneous product

Summary

It is clear that firms selling heterogeneous products are in a much better position than those selling homogeneous ones in terms of pricing strategies in response to exchange risk. Even so, for most producers, exposure to risk is significant which means that firms have to look beyond pricing responses to deal with it. What then can be done to reduce exposure to exchange risk? One possibility is the use of forecasts, and to understand the basis of these we need to know something about the causes of exchange rate changes.

Question

1. 'A firm selling a heterogeneous product has more discretion over the price it sets in foreign markets than one selling a homogeneous product.' Discuss.

7.3 Economic Fundamentals

There are a number of economic interrelationships involved in exchange rate determination. One useful approach is the four-way equivalence model outlined in Buckley (1992) and drawn in Figure 7.3. These relationships are now derived.

Interest rates and exchange rates

Assume an investor has £100 to invest for one year. He could invest it in say the UK or the USA. If he invests it in the UK his return is 100 (1 + r) where r is the domestic rate of interest. His dollar return from investing in the USA

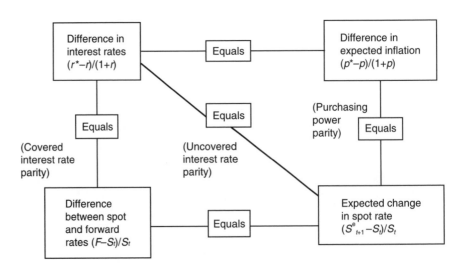

Figure 7.3 Equilibrium conditions in the foreign exchange markets

will be $100S_t(1 + r^*)$ where r^* is the American interest rate and $S_t =$ the current spot exchange rate in terms of dollars per pound. A UK investor will, however, be interested in the sterling return. Two approaches are possible. The first is that the investor could form an expectation of the future spot rate one year from now, S^e_{t+1}, and divide his dollar return by this.

He will be indifferent between investing in the UK or USA (assuming away the problem of risk) as long as:

$$100(1 + r) = \frac{100S_t(1 + r^*)}{S^e_{t+1}}$$

Cancelling out the 100 and rearranging terms, we get:

$$\frac{S^e_{t+1}}{S_t} = \frac{1 + r^*}{1 + r}$$

Taking $\frac{S_t}{S_t} = 1$ from the left-hand side of the equation and $\frac{1 + r}{1 + r} = 1$ from the right, we obtain:

$$\frac{S^e_{t+1} - S_t}{S_t} = \frac{r^* - r}{1 + r} \qquad (7.1)$$

This is **uncovered interest rate parity**.

Alternatively, our investor could use the forward market to make a contract today to sell his dollars for sterling one year from now. Let F be the rate he is quoted by the bank. In this case, he will be indifferent between investing in the UK and USA as long as:

$$100(1 + r) = \frac{100S_t(1 + r^*)}{F}$$

Rearranging terms as before:

$$\frac{F}{S_t} = \frac{r + r^*}{1 + r}$$

and

$$\frac{F - S_t}{S_t} = \frac{r^* - r}{1 + r} \qquad (7.2)$$

This is **covered interest rate parity** and unlike the uncovered rate involves no risk for the investor who in this case is comparing the known return in sterling from investing in the UK with the known return in sterling from investing in the USA. There is, however, the possibility that the investor could miss out on favourable currency movements.

Of course equations (7.1) and (7.2) imply that the difference between spot and forward rates should equal the difference between present and expected future spot rates, i.e. that:

$$\frac{F - S_t}{S_t} = \frac{S_{t+1}^e - S_t}{S_t} \tag{7.3}$$

If this did not apply, it would be expected that forward rates would adjust until it did.

Exchange rates and inflation

Assume a particular basket of goods sells for £750 in the UK and for $1,200 in the USA and that the $/£ exchange rate is 1.4. In this case, a trader could buy in the UK at £750 and sell in the USA at $1,050, thereby making a profit per basket of $150, in the absence of transport and insurance costs. This possibility for 'arbitrage' would mean that goods would be shipped from the UK to the USA unless the price rose in the UK and fell in the USA. This could be because of changes in the prices of domestically produced goods or because the demand for dollars to pay for British goods led to an appreciation of the pound. Either way, equilibrium will only be achieved when the prices in the two markets are the same i.e. when:

$$P^* = PS_t$$

or

$$\frac{P^*}{P} = S_t \tag{7.4}$$

It follows that changes in the prices of different countries' goods will lead to changes in their spot exchange rate.

If (7.4) holds in the present it should also hold in the future. Thus if p^* is the expected annual rate of inflation in the USA and p is the expected annual rate of inflation in the UK then the expected spot exchange rate between the countries one year from now should be:

$$S_{t+1}^e = \frac{P^*(1 + p^*)}{P(1 + p)} \tag{7.5}$$

It follows from (7.4) and (7.5) that:

$$\frac{S_{t+1}^e - S_t}{S_t} = \left[\frac{P^*(1 + p^*)}{P(1 + p)} - \frac{P^*}{P} \right] \Big/ \frac{P^*}{P}$$

So:

$$\frac{S_{t+1}^e - S_t}{S_t} = \frac{1 + p^*}{1 + p} - 1$$

Instead of -1 we can write $-\dfrac{(1 + p)}{(1 + p)}$ which is the same thing i.e.:

$$\frac{S_{t+1}^e - S_t}{S_t} = \frac{1 + p^*}{1 + p} - \frac{1 + p}{1 + p} = \frac{p^* - p}{1 + p} \tag{7.6}$$

This is called **purchasing power parity** and states that expected changes in exchange rates will reflect inflation differentials in respective countries.

Interest rates and inflation

Investors will be interested in real returns. If so, nominal interest rates should reflect inflation. Thus a domestic UK investor should be indifferent between a nominal return of 3 per cent if there is no inflation and a return of 9 per cent if inflation is 6 per cent. Similarly UK investors should be indifferent, *ceteris paribus*, between a nominal return of 3 per cent in the UK with no UK inflation and a return of 9 per cent in the USA if inflation is 6 per cent for, as we have seen, the exchange rate should adjust to make sure that by the time the money is changed back to pounds, its purchasing power will be the same. Thus the expected difference in inflation rates should equal the difference in nominal interest rates, i.e.:

$$\frac{p^* - p}{1 + p} = \frac{r^* - r}{1 + r} \tag{7.7}$$

This then completes our explanation of the relationships depicted in Figure 7.3. As an approximation, they may be written as:

$$r^* - r \simeq p^* - p \simeq \frac{F - S_t}{S_t} = \frac{S_{t+1}^e - S_t}{S_t} \tag{7.8}$$

as long as r and by implication p are small. Thus exchange rate movements and the difference between forward and spot rates should equal differences in inflation and nominal interest rates.

Of course there are many imperfections in the foreign exchange markets, some of them caused by government controls in particular countries, and they are, in any event, equilibrium conditions which may not and certainly do not apply necessarily in the short or even medium term.

They do, however, imply that particular factors will be influential in exchange rate movements. In particular, a relatively high rate of inflation in a particular currency is likely to lead to currency depreciation as would a deficit on the balance of payments possibly caused by such inflation. The latter might be caused by a too high level of home demand.

Also important will be the level of world demand and how changes in that level will impact on the particular commodities being traded by specific countries. If country A is producing goods which are increasingly demanded as world income grows, the currency of country A is likely to appreciate.

A further important factor is interest rates. The inference from both covered and uncovered interest rate parity is that a relatively high interest rate in country A would be balanced by an expected depreciating exchange rate. This may not apply in the short-run, when an increase in, say, UK interest rates relative to those of the USA should lead to an appreciation of the pound relative to the dollar as capital flows into the UK.

A final important influence is expectations and these can be used to explain the all too common fact that exchange rates often adjust to a greater extent than would be suggested by economic fundamentals. The latter point is emphasized by the fluctuation in the \$/£ exchange rate from 2.4 to just over 1.0 in the 1980s. The model outlined below can explain this and the different impact of interest rates in the long and short-run.

Complete models

Consider, for example, the case of a reduction in the money supply and assume that FOREX dealers operate on the principle of purchasing power parity (PPP). If so, they will now work out that the fall in the money supply should mean a fall in the price level and, given equation (7.4), an appreciation of the exchange rate. If they think the pound is *going to* appreciate they will buy pounds *now* and it will therefore appreciate. If prices are 'sticky' they will remain high for a while and, given the new lower money supply, this implies a relative shortage of money. Interest rates will now rise and induce more money to flow across the exchanges leading to a further appreciation of the currency in question. In other words it will, at least for a time, *overshoot* its long-term level. The position is illustrated in Figure 7.4.

Assume that the UK economy is in equilibrium at the time t_0 when the UK government reduces the money supply. Instead of settling at a new equilibrium at point C immediately the exchange rate moves to level B^1 before gradually depreciating to C^1 at time t_1.

Such overshooting does seem consistent with the facts. Note for example the fluctuations in the value of the dollar referred to above.

The impact of overshooting may well be long-term and in some cases irreversible. A rising exchange rate as in the above case leads to reduced price competitiveness in international markets and to a consequent loss of export markets and to import penetration. The appreciation of sterling in the

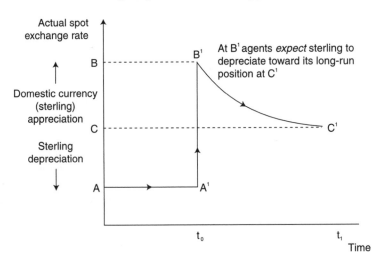

Figure 7.4 Exchange rate overshooting

period 1979–81, for example, contributed to a rapid fall of about 15 per cent in *manufacturing* output over the same period and to the subsequent reverse multiplier effects that led to a fall in *total* output of some 2–3 per cent over two years.

There are, however, some self-correcting mechanisms that can reverse the above decline in output, consequent on the overshooting in the exchange rate, though these appear to work slowly and Keynesians, at least, would argue that output does not fully attain its previous level. The mechanism is that as domestic demand falls in the recession this leads to increased unemployment and downward pressure on wages and hence on prices. In addition, lower domestic import prices consequent on the appreciation feed directly into business costs and lower prices. As domestic prices fall, this offsets the adverse competitiveness effects of the nominal appreciation, and net trade volume (i.e. exports less imports) begins to expand and output rises. As prices fall (or rise less fast), holders of financial assets which have interest rates that are sticky or zero (for example, current accounts, some bank and building society deposits) feel 'richer': the value of their assets rises, in terms of their purchasing power over goods. This appears to have a powerful positive impact on consumer spending and output.

However, a Keynesian-type supply-side effect has adverse consequences working via the productivity of the labour force. Older workers made redundant in the manufacturing sector may be unable or unwilling to retrain in the new expanding sectors (for example, health, business services, computers), while young potential entrants to the labour force may be permanently deterred from seeking employment because of the frustration in their unsuccessful search for what are perceived by them to be acceptable job offers. Hence the overall productivity of the potential labour force may fall and with it the economy's overall level of potential output. Thus the adverse consequences of overshooting on real output may be permanent.

Having looked at the economic fundamentals of exchange rate changes we must now return to the theme of what to do about them. One obvious possibility is the use of forecasts. These may be based on complex econometric models, and therefore the above fundamentals, or on more simple techniques. The latter are examined first of all.

Questions

1. Explain the terms 'spot' and 'forward' rate.
2. Explain the terms covered and uncovered interest rate parity.
3. How are forward rates calculated from spot rates given the information in the financial press? Calculate the $/£ exchange rate one month and three months forward in the following case:

Close	Spot rate One month: premium discount	Three months: premium discount
1.3075–1.3085	0.40–0.37 cents pm	1.03–0.98 cents pm

4. Your company has to make a US $0.5 million payment in one year's time. The dollars are available now. You decide to invest them for the year and are given the following information:

   - the US deposit rate is 8 per cent per annum;
   - the sterling deposit rate is 10 per cent per annum;
   - the spot exchange rate is $1.70/£; and
   - the one year forward rate is $1.62/£.

   (a) Where should your company invest for the better return?
   (b) Assuming that interest rates and spot exchange rates remain the same, what forward rate would yield a situation where one was indifferent as to whether one held pound or dollar deposits?
   (c) Assuming that the US dollar interest rate and the forward rates remain as above, where would you invest if the sterling deposit rate were 14 per cent per annum.
   (d) With the originally stated spot and forward rates, and the same dollar deposit rates what is the value of the sterling deposit rate that would make you indifferent as to whether you held pound or dollar assets?

5. What is the PPP theory of the relationship between prices and exchange rate determination?
6. Why might exchange rates overshoot?
7. How can rational expectations help us to understand short-run changes in exchange rates?
8. Interest rates on government bonds are 12 per cent in the UK and 10 per cent in the USA. Why might this be?

7.4 Exchange Rate Forecasts

Simple techniques are widely used for exchange rate forecasting so it is worth having a look at them in some detail.

Graphical methods

The use of graphical methods is usually referred to as chartism since those employing these methods use charts to plot exchange rate movements. Here a time series graph of the exchange rate is projected into the future as shown in Figure 7.5.

A relatively more sophisticated method of picking out turning-points on the 'chart' is to look at successive values of the change in the exchange rate, $(S_t - S_{t-1})$.

As an upper turning-point is approached (for example, B, Figure 7.5) then $(S_t - S_{t-1})$ gets smaller and is zero at the peak, before becoming negative. Thus, a decreasing value in successive periods for $(S_t - S_{t-1})$ might signify an imminent turning-point. However, chartism, even sophisticated chartism, is hazardous. For example, suppose the exchange rate path goes through a small 'step up' (for example, E-F-G, Figure 7.5). Here $(S_t - S_{t-1})$ approaches zero

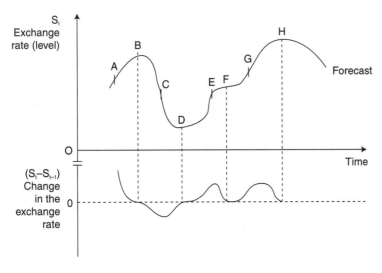

Figure 7.5 Forecasting the exchange rate by chartism methods

in successive time periods but S continues to rise in subsequent periods (to point H).

Looking at charts seems very simple. In practice, however, chartist projections may be based on considerably more complex analysis with computer programs used to give the forecast plots. Computers can also be programmed to give buy and sell prompts to FOREX dealers in certain circumstances. Suppose, for example, the $/£ exchange rate over the past year fluctuated consistently between 1.95 and 1.75. This would suggest that each time the rate dropped to 1.75 speculators or central banks considered the pound to be undervalued and bought pounds. Similarly every time the pound approached 1.95 it was generally regarded as overvalued and pounds were sold. In this way 1.95 and 1.75 may be considered *resistance* points.

If subsequently the exchange rate fell below 1.75, this would suggest that the perception of the value of the pound had changed. The chartist would now suspect that the exchange rate had broken out from the resistance level and might be expected to continue to fall until a new resistance level was reached.

A difficulty with all this is that since many chartists work on similar lines their predictions can be self-fulfilling. There may, therefore, be dramatic falls in the value of the currency once a resistance level has been reached. As we shall see below there are other reasons why this can occur. Despite the crudeness of the chartist approach it is extensively used both for exchange rates and share prices by a number of city forecasting firms, sometimes with a reasonable degree of success (Buckley, 1992).

Simplistic statistical models

The following simple statistical models have often been advocated for use by business forecasters:

(a) $S_t = S_{t-1}$ Random walk   (7.9)

(b) $S_t = F_{t-1}$ Forward rate   (7.10)

(c) $S_t = a_1 S_{t-1} + a_2 S_{t-2} + a_3 S_{t-3}$ Autoregressive   (7.11)

The random walk model (a) assumes that, in the absence of any more obvious alternatives, the exchange rate today is the best indicator for the next period. Alternatively the forward rate model (b) assumes that today's forward rate is the best predictor of the next period's spot rate. Finally, the autoregressive model (c) assumes that the next period's spot rate is a weighted average of past spot rates. The weights ai can be obtained by regression analysis. As we shall see below, there is some evidence that these simple models perform reasonably well.

Economic forecasting models

These are based upon the view that exchange rates are ultimately dependent on the economic fundamentals, previously discussed. The two basic alternatives are single equation and complete models.

Single equation models

Such models are represented by equations of the following type:

$$S = f\{(P \overset{-}{-} P^*), C \overset{+}{B}, (r \overset{+}{-} r^*)\}$$ (7.12)

where the signs are as indicated for S, measured in dollars per pound sterling. The *P*s are domestic and foreign price levels and *CB* = current account balance. Normally *CB* and $r-r^*$ would be considered as short-term influences on *S* with relative prices affecting the exchange rate in the long-term. There are some variations to this model. The above is a Keynesian version (e.g. the NIESR model) but a monetarist one would substitute money supply figures for relative prices. The model can be estimated by linear regression. One problem with it is that it requires the business forecaster to input his own guesses for the right-hand side variables in (7.8). Moreover no account is taken of the feedback effects of changes in the exchange rate on these right-hand side variables. Take, for example, an increase in the money supply. This would be expected to lead to an increase in $(P-P^*)$ and to a depreciation of the exchange rate. But this depreciation will in turn raise import prices and hence the domestic price level p and any change in the current account deficit will be reflected in changes in CB. A final problem is that no account is taken of the role of expectations, which as argued above are probably of some importance too in exchange rate determination.

Complete models

In such models, the exchange rate is part of a simultaneous equation system modelling the whole economy. Key assumptions are usually that goods prices are 'sticky' in the short-run, that capital flows are covered by uncovered interst rate parity and that expectations about the exchange rate do play an important role in determining current movements in the spot exchange rate. As seen above, such models are capable of explaining exchange rate overshooting.

Exchange rate forecast performance

Interestingly there is some evidence (Meese and Rogoff, 1983) that simple models perform well in relation to the more complex single equation econometric models and even in relation to complete macroeconomic models. Overall their results were relatively unfavourable to the econometric equations and frequently the 'best' forecasting equation was a no change random walk model. Similar results were found by Goodhart *et al.* (1992). Day-to-day and month-to-month changes in exchange rates are clearly more volatile than movements in economic fundamentals would suggest (Taylor, 1995). Certainly, there is little evidence of purchasing power parity at least over the short to medium term (Buckley, 1992). An interesting recent study is by Pilbeam (1994) who examines how three groups of investors applying simple decision rules would have fared in the foreign exchange markets from 1974 to 1991. He examined four bilateral sterling exchange rates and found that chartist models performed slightly better than 'simpleton' ones including random walk which in turn did better than economic fundamentalist ones. However, allowing for variability of returns, a random walk forecaster may have done best.

It also seems to be the case that professional commercial forecasters do not appear to yield, on average, better forecasts of the spot rate over one to twelve months than one would obtain using the forward rate, although individual organizations can do relatively well.

Either way it seems clear, that economic fundamentals do not appear to be accurate predictors of short-run changes in exchange rates. An explanation may be found in the impact of information or 'news' or exchange rate changes.

Up to this point we have confined our analysis to a discussion of the 'fundamental' variables that are thought to influence exchange rates (for example, relative prices, current balance, interest rates). However, as argued above, day-to-day and month-to-month changes in spot rates appear to be more volatile than would be predicted using equations involving changes in these fundamental variables. Does this imply that foreign exchange, FOREX dealers create short-term instability of exchange rates? A useful starting-point in examining this question is to reconsider the uncovered interest parity relationship (equation 7.2):

$$\frac{S_{t+1}^e - S_t}{S_t} = \frac{r^* - r}{1 + r} \tag{7.13}$$

Suppose there is an unexpected increase in the foreign interest rate, between t and $t + 1$. The *actual* spot rate of the domestic currency would then depreciate below the level expected before this new information (or 'news') became available. Such 'jumps' take place instantaneously as FOREX dealers alter their quoted spot price over the telephone. In contrast, consider an announced increase in the USA (foreign) interest rate to become effective in one month's time or, more realistically, a guess by FOREX dealers that the policy of the Federal Reserve Board will be to reduce monetary growth in one month's time. In both cases FOREX dealers react immediately and mark sterling down, as agents attempt to get rid of sterling assets today. When the US interest rate alters in one month's time the spot rate will remain unchanged since the anticipated event will have already been incorporated in their view of the appropriate exchange rate. This highlights the different response of the exchange rate to anticipated and unanticipated events.

The exchange rate may 'jump' before the actual causal event takes place if the latter is anticipated, while unanticipated events may lead to major revisions in expectations and volatile jumps in the exchange rate from week to week. Though such volatility affects the usefulness of macroeconomic forecasting models in the short-run they may, of course, be of some use for long-run planning. Certainly there is some evidence that economic fundamentals do affect exchange rates in the long-run (Taylor, 1995).

Summary

Exchange rates are so difficult to forecast that the businessman would be unwise to rely too heavily on any predictions. 'Exchange rate overshooting' in particular is far from a theoretical curiosum. Exchange rate forecasting may be hazardous, whatever method is used, and perhaps the major useful practical element that emerges is the possibility of assessing alternative scenarios using a complete macro model, in which the behaviour of the exchange rate is usually of crucial importance. Some ideas of the sensitivity of business decisions on pricing, output and asset diversification to changes in the exchange rate and other exogenous variables (for example, world demand) can then be ascertained and used in the firm's planning process. The degree of uncertainty can then be crudely quantified and assessed and, if nothing else, the businessman can hold a coherent view of future exchange rate movements given his assumption about the future course of government policy and external events. These issues are discussed in later chapters. For the moment we turn to specific strategies to deal with exchange rate risk.

Questions

1. 'Evidence suggests that simple models for forecasting exchange rates perform as well as complex ones.' Discuss.
2. 'Chartism, even sophisticated Chartism, has no basis in rational behaviour and hence should be treated with care and avoided where possible.' Discuss.
3. What are resistance levels?
4. What is a random walk model?

5. 'Exchange rates are impossible to predict in the short-run as they bear little relationship to economic fundamentals.' Discuss.
6. Explain the difference between a) single equation models, and b) complete macroeconomic models in forecasting exchange rates.
7. To what extent does purchasing power parity apply in practice?

7.5 Risk Avoidance

Use of the forward market

There are two main types of 'deal' on the FOREX market. The first is the 'spot' rate which is the exchange rate quoted immediately for delivery of the currency to the buyer two working days later. The second is the forward rate which is the guaranteed price at which the buyer will take delivery of currency at some future period. This may be one month, two months, three months, six months or a year and in exceptional circumstances three to five years ahead. The market-makers in the FOREX market are mainly the large commercial banks.

The forward rate may be higher or lower than the spot rate, reflecting interest rate differentials between respective countries over the length of the contract, as outlined above.[3] The use of the forward rate eliminates risk from future exchange rate changes since the rate is *agreed* today even though the transaction takes place in the future. This does not, of course, mean that our corporate treasurer will necessarily use the forward market. One reason is that in addition to the above quotation he will also pay a commission to the FOREX dealer. More important, however, is that the firm has the option to take an 'open' or risky position if it so chooses.

The individual firm is not, of course, bound by the expectations of the market. If the corporate treasurer of the firm thinks that for example, the dollar will appreciate in excess of interest rate differentials, he or she would be more likely to invest in the USA. Quite simply the corporate treasurer will now expect the money that he earns there to convert into more pounds in the future. Similarly, a UK business person expecting to be paid for an export order to the US in three months' time with the price already fixed in dollars will be likely to take an open position if he or she holds the same expectations.

Most of the time, however, firms will be likely to use the forward market. The reason is that it completely avoids exchange risk to the importer or exporter. The importer knows the price he or she will have to pay and the exporter what he or she will receive. It will, therefore, be attractive to risk averse firms. How much use a particular firm will make of the forward market will in any event also depend on the time interval between receipts and payments and the countries in which it does business. The forward markets are most useful for short-term transactions in the world's major currencies.

Use of option contracts

Option contracts are forward contracts in which the customer has the *option* to invoke the contract either at any date from that of the contract being made to a specified future date or between any two specified dates in the future.

For example, such contracts are useful for situations when a business is not sure of the exact date on which it will want to buy or sell currency, and they avoid the necessity for having to extend forward contracts (which can be expensive on a short-term basis). The benefit to the firm is that foreign exchange risk can be covered with certainty even when there is uncertainty about the precise date of the transaction. There is however a 'cost' to the firm since it has to pay a premium in order to 'buy' the option contract from the dealer. If the firm's foreign currency receipts arrive on the expected date then the corporate treasurer undertakes only the forward market transaction and does not 'exercise' (i.e. 'cash in' his or her right to) the option. However, if the receipts arrive a little later than anticipated the corporate treasurer can 'exercise' the option to purchase the currency at the pre-arranged fixed price (known as the strike price).

Hedging

In certain circumstances it is impossible to use the forward market to mini-mize exposure to risk. Where, for example, there is no forward market for funds, say for five years ahead a corporate treasurer can effectively hedge by using the foreign securities market (i.e. loan and asset purchases). For exam-ple, suppose a UK firm is to receive $10,000 in five years' time. If $r^* = 0.1$, the annual rate of interest on an American bank loan, then a loan of $10,000/(1 + r^*)^5 = \$6209.2$ will accumulate debt interest of exactly $\$(10,000 - 6209.2)$ over five years. The UK firm's $10,000 receipt in five years' time will pay off the principal and interest on a dollar loan of $6209.2. But the $6209.2 received today can be immediately switched into sterling in the spot market. Hence although the $10,000 accrues in five years' time, the UK firm knows exactly how much sterling it represents today. The possibility clearly exists, then, of reducing exchange rate risk by borrowing in the foreign currency against known future receipts in the foreign currency.

Risk-spreading

It is generally accepted that it is not a good idea to put all your eggs into one basket, and this prompts the question as to whether our corporate treasurer could reduce the firm's exposure to exchange risk for any given expected return by taking an open position in a number of currencies. To start the ball rolling consider a highly simplified case where our UK treasurer transfers £10,000 into a yen current account earning zero interest and expects the £/yen rate to remain constant. The expected return is £10,000. If, however, there is a 50 per cent change in the value of the yen against sterling, then the sterling value of the firm's overseas asset changes by £5,000, a high degree of variability. As an alternative investment strategy consider holding £5,000 each in yen and dollars where again we assume the investor expects zero change in the two bilateral rates against sterling. The expected return is again £10,000. Suppose, however, that the corporate treasurer has observed that in the past whenever the yen appreciates, the dollar always depreciates against sterling by an equal per centage amount (i.e. the correlation coefficient R between two currencies equals -1). If this condition prevails in the future, then, it turns out that the variability in his *sterling return* is zero, i.e. whatever the firm gains on its yen assets it loses on its dollar assets. In fact, even if the two currencies tend to move in the same direction, (but are not perfectly positively correlated) then in this two-asset case there is still some reduction in the overall risk if the portfolio is 'diversified' into the two currencies. It therefore appears that, if our fund manager can invest in a basket of currencies, particularly with some that have negative correlation (covariances) this will minimize the riskiness attached to the sterling value of the firm's total assets.

In practice the overseas investment decision involves considerations other than simply exchange risk. The choice may involve a UK corporate treasurer investing in an 'own currency risky asset', for example, in a US government bond or equity. Here the dollar price of the asset is uncertain if sold on the open market before its maturity date.

The general 'strength' of the foreign economy will influence sentiment in its equity market and hence price quotations on the stock exchange and may also effect its exchange rate in the same direction. This increases the potential variability in the sterling return. A mix of foreign equity and foreign government bonds (which are less influenced by the State of the economy) in a particular currency helps to minimize exposure to risk in this instance. Thus a corporate treasurer might engage in a sequential approach to portfolio management. He or she might first, choose the optimum spread between currencies and, second, diversify by type of asset in any one currency.

In the latter respect, liquidity will be an important consideration. The more 'liquid' a financial asset, the more easily it may be switched into a means of payment without incurring high transactions costs (for example, brokerage and banking charges) or risk of capital loss because its market price is uncertain at the time of sale (for example, as with equities, government bonds). Cash and chequing accounts are highly liquid as are overdraft facilities for large companies. Short-term assets such as ninety-day certificates of deposit, Treasury Bills and Commercial Bills are also highly liquid on this definition. Government bonds (gilt-edged stock), preference shares and equity involve higher transaction costs and greater risk of a capital loss (or gain) when sold and hence are deemed to be less liquid.

A multinational company may face an uncertain net inflow or outflow of funds on its profit and loss account and will need to act quickly to provide 'cash funds'. In any one currency, firms will therefore hold a portfolio of assets throughout the liquidity spectrum. Then, an outflow of dollar payments, say, by a UK firm may be met either by running down dollar chequing accounts, by increasing dollar overdrafts, or by selling short-term dollar assets (for example, US commercial bills) or long-term assets (for example, US government bonds) that are either near to maturity (and hence have a price close to their par or redemption value) or appear to command a favourable price in the market.

Investment in foreign subsidiaries

Though there are many considerations involved in the costly business of setting up overseas subsidiaries they do have a clear *financial* advantage in the avoidance of exchange risk. This is that production in a particular foreign country usually involves a close matching of receipts and disbursements in that particular foreign currency. Take, for example, the case of the European operations of the Ford Motor Company. It produces and sells in a number of European countries most of the currencies of which are closely aligned in the European Monetary System. Ford can, therefore, borrow in say Deutschmarks, pay German production workers in Deutschmarks and sell cars in Germany and throughout Europe with little exposure to exchange risk.

The main problem with setting up subsidiaries in addition to the cost already referred to is the remission of surplus profits to the parent company. The parent then has the problem as outlined above of the optimum allocation of funds between currencies. The Eurocurrency markets (which include US

Box 7.2 UK foreign investment

The UK is now the most open economy in the world for inward investment, for, in the decade 1980–90, it comprised 1.75 per cent of GDP compared to around 1.4 per cent in The Netherlands and 1.1 per cent in Switzerland (Wallace, 1996). In the USA and France it comprised between 0.5 and 1 per cent of GDP while in Sweden, Italy, Germany, Spain and Japan it comprised 0.4 per cent or less. It is not, however, all one-way traffic, for the UK is also the biggest overseas investor at about 2.75 per cent of GDP, again followed by The Netherlands and Switzerland. Sweden comes next followed by Japan and Spain but, over the decade, France and Germany had only around one-third as much outward investment as the UK. Since then, high production costs in Germany, in particular, may well have changed matters somewhat though both outward and inward investment remain bouyant in the UK. In total some 40 per cent of Japanese and American investment in Europe has come to the latter. The arrival of Nissan and Toyota has revived UK car production while Sony, Toshiba and others have turned the UK into a net exporter of colour televisions some of which now go to the Far East.

In total foreign direct investment from OECD countries grew at a rate of 15 per cent per year between 1985 and 1994.

Of course, such inward investment has resulted from globalization of markets and also from the development of trading blocks such as the European Union as well as a desire to minimize exchange rate risk.

dollars) provide a relatively cheap and quick way of switching funds between currencies, and therefore subsidiaries, and hence holding a basket of Euro-currencies minimizes exposure to exchange risk while maintaining a high degree of liquidity.

Summary

Large multinationals, even those with a number of foreign subsidiaries, cannot avoid the problem of allocating some of their surplus funds in 'risky' assets. They may be risky in terms of capital value, in terms of exchange risk and, where setting up subsidiaries or take-overs of foreign firms are involved, in terms of a whole host of production, marketing and managerial information costs. The decision to invest in foreign 'real assets' may involve extensive market analysis of the foreign economy in general and also of particular markets (for example, for sales, labour, supplier companies) as well as of political risk. Ultimately shareholders of the parent company will require dividend payments in the domestic currency and these will depend in part on movements in the bilateral rates between the domestic currency and the set of foreign currencies. Members of a corporate finance department will there-fore need to trade off the liquidity, expected return and the various forms of risk of which exchange risk is an important part in deciding the optimal allocation of funds across assets in different currencies.

We have tried to develop the basic framework for analysing these problems from the point of view of the individual business person in either a small company or a large multinational. Actual investment decisions require rela-tively complex decision rules (as well as good hunches!) but broadly speaking they involve factors discussed in the simple cases above. We hope therefore that the reader is now aware of the issues to be tackled by the corporate strategy department and the small exporter alike in overseas pricing, sales, production and portfolio investment decisions.

7.6 CONCLUSION

The exchange rate impinges on the cost and production decisions of firms, since changes in the real exchange rate can have powerful effects on price competitiveness and sales volume both abroad and in the home market.

Exchange rates are so difficult to forecast that business people must hedge against exchange risk whenever possible and choose a portfolio of foreign assets to reduce risk to an acceptable level while earning a sufficient 'return' and maintaining adequate liquidity in foreign assets.

Questions

1. What do you understand by the terms 'spot' and 'forward' rate? How are they presented in the financial press?
2. How can a firm seek to minimize exchange risk?

3. What is meant by hedging? When and how is it used in foreign exchange dealings and transactions involving foreign currencies (assets)?
4. How far do operations in the forward (FOREX) market safeguard a business in ensuring the viability of a contract with foreign partners?
5. Explain the basic elements behind currency options and currency swaps.
6. Given that using the forward market reduces exchange rate risk, why don't all importers and exporters use it?
7. A Mexican businessman has to make a payment in US dollars one year from now to an American company for machine tools he has ordered. He is worried that the peso will depreciate relative to the dollar. Show how he can hedge his risk without using a forward market.

Notes

1. The exchange rate, S, is quoted here in 'indirect' terms of $/£. An increase in S in this case means an appreciation of the pound and a depreciation of the dollar. The opposite would apply if S were quoted in 'direct' terms of £/$. Conventions differ on this. In the UK, the indirect quote is used whereas in the USA, for example, the direct quote is adopted.
2. The pivoting of the new demand and MR curves can be explained by the use of simple calculus. Assume a linear demand curve:

$$Q = a - bP_f S/P^*$$

where P_f = price in pounds of the good and P^* = price in dollars.

The slope:

$$dQ/dP_f = -\frac{S_b}{P^*}$$

so:

$$\frac{dP_f}{dQ} = -\frac{P^*}{S_b}$$

This is the slope of the demand curve as drawn. The higher is S, the smaller is the slope which pivots from point a on the Q axis. The slope of the MR curve is twice the slope of the demand curve.

3. Forward rates are often quoted as a premium or discount on 'spot' rates. If the dollar, for example, is at a 'premium' three months forward of 0.32 cents and the spot rate is 1.5284($/£), then the three months forward rate is 1.5252($/£).

The financial environment $\boxed{8}$

All that glistens is not gold. Often have you heard that told.

(William Shakespeare)

8.1 INTRODUCTION

The previous chapter discussed the factors influencing the allocation of funds between various foreign assets. We now concentrate on the determination of domestic interest rates, although clearly the interdependence between domestic and foreign financial markets cannot be ignored.

We begin with a look at the importance of interest rates to business in section 8.2 before turning to a discussion of economic fundamentals. This requires a look at the returns on different types of assets, the determination of relative interest rates and the determination of interest rates in general. Of particular relevance here is the role of the Government, working through the Central Bank, on financial markets. Both monetary and fiscal policy affect certain key interest rates including the short rate on ninety-one-day Treasury bills or commercial bills and the long rate on gilt-edged stock. Changes in these two key rates feed through the whole of the financial system and lead to changes in many other interest rates. Thus, if the Central Bank operates on short rates it may be able to effect long rates. The latter then influence equity prices and hence the real investment decisions of firms. The impact of foreign interest rates, perceptions of risk and herding behaviour on domestic interest rates are also discussed. We then look at interest rate forecasts and strategies to deal with risk.

8.2 THE IMPACT OF INTEREST RATES ON BUSINESS

Movements in interest rates have a direct and important impact upon the firm. First and most obvious, actual changes and expected future movements in interest rates influence a firm's *real* investment decisions. This applies to longer-term projects such as expansion of existing plant, the purchase of new machinery or a new vehicle fleet as well as short-term investment, such as deciding what quantity of stocks of raw materials or finished goods to hold.

Interest rates may influence both the amount of real investment and its timing. As far as the amount is concerned, the situation can be illustrated in terms of the internal rate of return (IRR) defined as the discount factor which makes the NPV (see Chapter 5) equal to zero. Thus the higher the NPV the higher the IRR on the project. The IRR curve can be considered as the demand curve for capital and will be downward-sloping reflecting the fact that the most profitable projects will be undertaken first (see Figure 8.1). The firm will undertake investments until the IRR on the marginal project is equal to the cost of borrowing the money to pay for it. This is the marginal cost of capital, MCC. The latter is assumed to rise as the risk of default will increase as more projects are undertaken. Equilibrium is at V_0. An increase in interest rates shifts the marginal cost of capital upwards and there is a new equilibrium at V_1 involving a lower level of investment.

On the question of the timing of investment, if the business person believes that interest rates will fall in the near future it will be advantageous for the firm to postpone its purchase of capital equipment in order to obtain more favourable terms.

In principle, real investment should respond to changes in real interest rates, that is, the nominal per centage interest rate, r, less the expected rate of price inflation. If inflation is expected to be 10 per cent per annum over the life of the investment project and the cost of borrowing is $r = 12$ per cent per annum, then the investment project should be just as profitable as when $r = 3$ per cent per annum and inflation is 1 per cent per annum because the real interest is 2 per cent in both cases. This result is incorporated in the NPV formula for investment since, if nominal returns provide the numerator, then the nominal interest rate is used to discount future receipts in the denominator, thus cancelling out the effect of inflation on the NPV of the project. However, because nominal interest rates can move independently of inflation, a change in the former often implies a change in real interest rates and hence in the NPV of the project and the investment decision.

Changes in interest rates may also influence the liquidity and hence poten-

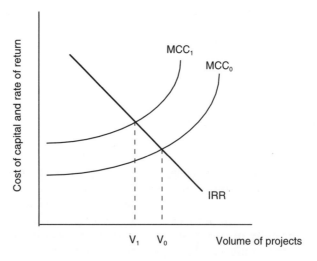

Figure 8.1 The volume of investment undertaken by a firm

Box 8.1 Interest rates and investment

Classical economists argue that investment should be highly interest elastic since lower real interest rates would mean that more investment projects would be profitable using discounting methods of investment appraisal if interest rates were low than if interest rates were high. However, most UK studies have failed to show a close relationship, indeed investment seems to be highly interest inelastic. Turner (1989), for example, found only a weak relationship between the real rate of interest and investment in plant and machinery. Keynes (1936) view was that investment was largely influenced by 'animal spirits' for which we can substitute business confidence. Thus if business people think it is a good time to invest they will do so, perhaps because their view of the likely nominal and real returns over the life of a project will be boosted. Thus, the numerator rather than the denominator of the NPV calculation may be crucial.

Even so, one study of the UK and other countries did find that high real interest rates depressed investment and output from 1990 to 1993 (Osler, 1994). According to Easton (1990), however, the major impact in the UK is on the housing market.

tial solvency of firms. If a firm has a high level of income gearing (i.e. net interest payments on short-term liabilities as a proportion of revenue or profits), then a rise in interest rates will increase interest payments and, if a cushion of liquid assets is not readily available, the firm may experience cash flow problems and may possibly have to go into liquidation.

Finally, when a firm undertakes a large investment project, such as building a new UK plant, then the mix of finance will be partly influenced by the relative interest cost of various forms of finance. For example, what proportion of funds should come from retained profits, bank advances, issues of commercial bills, debenture or equity? This decision depends upon the business person's view of current interest rates and share price trends. Even if a firm uses retained profits as a source of finance the cost of such funds is not zero, but the interest the firm could make by investing the funds elsewhere (e.g. in a deposit account). Because of the low transactions costs of bank lending (which is now available on a longer-term basis of up to twenty years as well as short-term overdrafts) and issuing commercial bills, these 'outside' sources of finance are used more frequently than costly debenture and equity issues. It is perhaps also worth noting that some firms expand by take-overs. They borrow funds in order to purchase the shares of other firms whose shares they believe are undervalued, given the value of the real capital equipment and goodwill of the firm under threat of take-over. However, this is not an expansion in aggregate investment in the economy, but merely a change in ownership and control though it could, of course, lead to higher aggregate investment in the future. It might be argued that a lower general level of interest rates encourages borrowing for such take-over bids (for example, Guinness for Distillers in the UK in 1986).

In the USA in the 1980s a number of take-over bids were financed by issuing fixed-interest 'junk' bonds to investors. The idea was that, after the take-over, the assets of the firm could be quickly sold off and the funds from this 'asset stripping' used to buy back some or all of the high-risk, high-interest bonds. However, for some time after the take-over, the purchasers of the firm would have to finance high interest payments on the junk bonds as such firms were highly geared and the failure to do so resulted in numerous bankruptcy proceedings in the USA.

It seems, therefore, that interest rates can have a very significant impact on business and we now examine them in detail.

Questions

1. Why should a rise in interest rates cause a reduction in investment? Would this still be true in a firm which financed all of its investment out of retained earnings?
2. Explain why the average cost of capital can be affected by the proportion of fixed interest finance used by a firm.
3. Why may take-over activity be greater when interest rates are relatively low?
4. What are junk bonds?

8.3 ECONOMIC FUNDAMENTALS

The main purpose of this section is to explain how interest rates are determined. It is first necessary, however, to look at the returns on different types of asset.

Relative interest rates and yields

If an asset such as a three-month bill is held to maturity a sensible measure of the return is the interest rate or 'yield to maturity' expressed at an annual rate. Thus, if one purchases a pure discount bill (i.e. one that pays no coupon) with three months to maturity with a redemption value of £100, at a market price of £97, then the yield to maturity is $r = [(100 - 97)/97] \times (12/3) \times 100$ per cent = 12.37 per cent per annum. (Note that, by convention, the 'yield' uses the market price of 97 in the denominator.) This is commonly referred to as the interest rate on the bill.

Now consider a bond with two years to maturity with a purchase price of P_B = £200. For purely illustrative purposes, suppose this bond pays out £110 in the first year and £121 in the second year and that is all. These known periodic payments are referred to as coupon payments on the bond. To calculate the yield to maturity on the bond, R at an annual rate, we use the NPV formula:

$$P_B = 200 = \frac{110}{(1 + R)} + \frac{121}{(1 + R)^2}$$

The value of R that equates the purchase price (£200) with the discounted present value of future coupon payments (£110 and £121) is by convention the yield to maturity. Here $R = 0.1$ or 10 per cent per annum. The investor can then loosely compare the annual yield over two years on the bond with the yield over one year on the bill r. Clearly, what happens to short-term (i.e. one-year bill) rates in the second year is of importance here and this aspect is dealt with when discussing the term structure of interest rates, below.

More typically bonds carry a specific coupon payment related to the nominal or 'par' price of the bond. Most UK government bonds or gilts as they are called are of this type. Thus £100 nominal government stock might have a fixed coupon payment of £12. In that case, if the price paid for the stock is £100 and does not change, the rate of interest is, of course, 12 per cent.

While the coupon payments on a bond are known with certainty over the remaining life of the bond, this is not the case for equities or common stocks. These assets usually pay a dividend, but the amount of the dividend is uncertain and depends in part upon the future level of profits. Hence it would be difficult to calculate a meaningful measure of the yield to maturity. In any case, there are several problems with the yield to maturity measure of the return, even for a bond. The most obvious is that it assumes a 'holding period' equal to the remaining life of the bond (i.e. until its redemption date) and the investor may have a shorter holding period. If the expected holding period is less than the life of the asset, then it makes more sense, particularly for long bonds, debentures and equities, to take account of expected capital gains over the holding period. Hence the holding period yield, *HPY*, is defined as:

$$HPY = [P_{t+1}^e - P_t + D_{t+1}]100/P_t$$

where P_t = purchase price of the asset; P_{t+1}^e = expected price at the end of the (fixed and arbitrary) holding period (e.g. one year); and D_{t+1} = any dividend or other payments made over the holding period. Thus, a corporate bond purchased for £90 with an expected dividend payment of £10 and an expected end-year price of £95 has a holding period yield of 16.7 per cent per annum. The latter is made up of an expected capital gain of 5.6 per cent and a dividend yield (D/P) 100 = 11.1 per cent.

There are, then, different types of asset and different ways of calculating the return. We now turn to the interesting question of differences in returns.

In general the rate of return on an asset is determined by the risk involved in holding it and this can be a function of time or the nature of the asset in question. Taking the nature of assets first, a key factor will be the ease with which such assets can be turned into money.

Thus, highly liquid assets such as chequeing accounts tend to earn zero or low interest, short-term marketable assets such as commercial and three month local authority bills earn slightly more interest and long-term marketable assets, such as gilts, earn more again because their market price, if sold before the redemption date, is uncertain. Finally, debentures and equity, which have highly volatile market prices depending upon the actual and expected profitability of particular companies, earn an even higher return. At any point in time, a set of interest differentials will be established between bills and bonds, based on supply and demand in these markets. There will also be a differential between the HPY on government bonds, corporate bonds and equities, reflecting the different perceived risk characteristics of these assets. In 'normal' periods new flows on to the market (for example, via pension funds) will largely be allocated in much the same proportion as previous flows (Friedman, 1977) and are unlikely to alter existing differentials radically.

The time element can best be examined by looking at a particular asset such as bonds. The relationship between the short rate, r_t, and the current long-term rate, R_t, on bonds is known as the term structure of interest rates and gives rise to the yield curve. This shows the relationship between the interest rate on a bond (more precisely, the yield to maturity) and its time to maturity. Normally, the curve slopes upwards (AA in Figure 8.2) and becomes flatter as the time to maturity lengthens. A yield curve refers to a particular point in time (i.e. interest rates on a specific day) and the whole curve may shift up or down as the general level of all interest rates alters (BB in Figure 8.2). The upward slope of the yield curve indicates, for example, that bonds with, say, twenty years to maturity will command a higher interest rate than those with one or two years to maturity.

There are, however, circumstances in which the yield curve can slope downwards, a situation which occurs when future short rates are expected to be lower than the current short rate. This might be the case if inflation is expected to fall in the future as this will be reflected in lower future expected short rates. Also, if the monetary authorities use high short-term interest rates to deflate the economy (as in the UK in 1990–1) and this policy is expected to be reversed in the future, then future short-term rates are expected to fall and, therefore, long rates will be below short rates. The reason is that investors will try to lock into present high interest rates by buying 'long' now. That drives up the price of long-term bonds, thereby depressing the yield.

Such situations are, however, rare for long bonds carry additional risk relative to shorts and to bills. First, unless held to maturity their market price

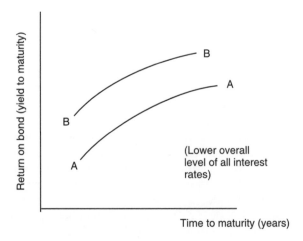

Figure 8.2 The yield curve

is uncertain. Second, even if held to maturity the real value of the interest payments, after deducting for inflation, may be far more uncertain on bonds with a long period to maturity because of uncertainty over future inflation levels.

It should be emphasized that rates of interest on non-marketable assets such as building society deposits will also move with market rates to preserve differentials. For example, if local authority bill rates rise, and people begin switching out of bank and building society deposits into bills, these latter institutions will raise the rate on their deposits, for, if they fail to raise rates, they will have to contract their lucrative lending operations on bank and mortgage advances. However, as banks and building societies are now paying higher rates on deposits, to remain solvent or keep profits high they must raise the interest rate on new and existing advances. Hence changes in market rates spread to rates on non-marketable assets and liabilities. The spread between a bank's borrowing rate and its lending rate will vary depending upon the profitability of the bank and the economic cycle. In times of recession, when lending to companies is riskier and, perhaps, bank profits are low, the bank may widen the margin between its lending and borrowing rates.

The HPYs on bonds and equities will also tend to move together as investors buy and sell the two assets in order to (largely) preserve the HPY

Box 8.2 Interest rates over time

In the sping of 1996, **nominal interest rates** in the UK were 6.25 per cent, a figure which was low by standards of the 1970s and 1980s but which was very high compared with earlier periods. The rate on long-term bonds rose to a crisis level of 6.3 per cent in 1797 and 1798 when the Napoleonic Wars threatened the survival of an independent UK state but fell almost continuously over the next century to a low of 2.25 per cent during 1896–8. After the First World War they were just over 5.25 per cent but by the mid-1930s were again less than 3. Similar levels were achieved after the Second World War.

Of course, the differences between the post-1970 period and before is explained by the different inflationary expectations, for before the Second World War there were periods when prices rose and when they fell. After the War price increases were the norm, and after 1970 they were rapid. The experience of the next two decades still haunts policy-makers today, even though inflation rates are now back to pre-war levels, not just in the UK but on a global scale. Some commentators argue that inflation has been permanently squeezed from the system so that there is no need for the high **real interest rates** currently prevailing. According to Bootle (1996a,1996b) there will be a gradual realization, not only in financial markets but in business and society at large, that the fundamental assumption that has underlain their economic lives for sixty years – perpetual inflation – no longer applies. They face a wholly new set of questions about how to prosper without it.

differentials between them (assuming no change in the perceived riskiness of the two types of asset).

The businessman must continually be aware of the flows of funds through the market and will no doubt gain insights into short-term movements in relative rates and prices from the financial press and City contacts.

It should now be clear to the reader that a change in one financial market will have, via the above mechanisms, a ripple effect throughout the financial system. A major and frequent external source of changes in financial markets is operations by the Central Bank in pursuit of its monetary, fiscal or exchange-rate policies. How do such policies affect interest rates and hence the investment decisions of firms? It is to this interaction between the Central Bank and the financial markets that we now turn.

Interest rate determination

Let us assume that the Government wishes to expand the school building programme while all other items of government expenditure remain constant. It could, of course, simply print more banknotes to pay for the expansion but let us assume that it has a money supply target which negates this approach. It must, therefore, borrow the money to pay for the expansion and it does so by instructing the Central Bank to sell more bills or bonds. Normally, the Central Bank tends to operate mainly at the short end of the market when setting their monetary stance, buying or selling vast quantities of three-month Treasury and commercial bills, some of which have only weeks or days to their maturity date. In contrast, long-term operations involving gilts or government bonds are only undertaken when demand is favourable. Assume a £1 billion increase in government expenditure is to be recouped by the sale of extra Treasury bills. The market price of bills falls to encourage additional purchasers and hence short-term interest rates rise. The commercial banks initially lose bank deposits and to stem the loss the banks may then raise the interest rate on wholesale deposits and bank advances, and may also try to sell bills, to obtain cash to replenish their depleted reserves. The ripple effect outlined above now proceeds through the financial system.

People will begin to switch funds out of low-yield building society deposits into high-yield bank deposits and to counter this loss of business, the building societies will raise both their deposit and mortgage advance rates.

The higher rate on bills will lead some people to sell longer-term bonds (e.g. gilt-edged stock) in order to switch into high-yield bills. However, this causes bond prices to fall and hence long interest rates, or more precisely the yields to maturity, R (equation 8.1), to rise. In addition, the holding period yield, HPY, on bonds may rise as the current price has fallen and the expected future price remains unchanged. Hence people will also now find it profitable to switch out of debentures and equity into high-yield long-term bonds. This leads to a fall in equity prices and a rise in their HPY. Thus, we see that a whole chain of interest-rate increases and a fall in equity prices has followed the initial rise in bill rates engineered by the Central Banks' open market operation. The absolute level of all interest rates rises. Bond and equity prices fall so that the HPY on these assets is brought back to equilibrium and any HPY differential is maintained. This is illustrated in the case of the yield curve (Figure 8.2) with the shift from AA to BB.

The yield curve indicates that the authorities, by manipulating short rates, may have direct leverage over long rates on government stock. A rise in short rates may lead to an upward shift of the yield curve, a rise in long rates and a fall in bond prices. Lower bond prices today with unchanged expectations imply a higher HPY on bonds and hence a switch out of equities into bonds. Equity prices therefore fall until HPY rises in line with that on bonds. Hence, because long government bonds are reasonably close substitutes for debentures and equities, changes in government bond rates also influence debenture and equity returns.

Lower interest rates on gilt-edged stock, for example, imply a lower expected HPY. Equities and debentures now appear relatively more attractive and increased purchases lead to a rise in their market price. This makes it cheaper for firms to float new issues as they can obtain more cash per share issued. Hence the authorities, by operating on short rates, may influence a whole range of long rates of return, for example, on gilts and in a less predictable fashion influence the market price of debentures, preference shares and equities, and hence the cost of finance for firms raising money on the stock exchange.

We also noted above that the Central Bank's open market operations lead to changes in the cost of non-marketable assets such as the rate on bank advances. Hence, the Central Bank also has an indirect effect on the cost of finance for firms and this leads to changes in stocks of raw materials, finished goods and work in progress and in fixed investment in plant, machinery, buildings and vehicles. Thus, fiscal policy can influence aggregate demand via its effect on the general level of a wide range of interest rates.

The 'ripple effect' through the financial system outlined above originated from a need to finance increased government borrowing. It could also, of course, have arisen from monetary or exchange rate policy. If, for example, the Government wished to reduce the money supply or to raise interest rates it could again do so by selling more government bills with exactly the same result.

It should be emphasized that announced changes in government policy may have an immediate effect on interest rates. Assume, for example, the Government announces a cut in welfare payments over the next year or an increased money supply target. If investors have rational expectations they will anticipate less government borrowing and higher bill and bond prices. They, therefore, buy bills and bonds *now* with the result that bill and bond prices rise *now*. Thus rational expectations bring forward in time the effect of any announced policy changes. The lesson for the manager if rational expectations apply is to note the speed with which the market reacts to changes in or 'news' about new policies. Interest rate changes may precede the actual event that causes the change!

To summarize, the yield curve shows that the authorities can influence long rates via their operations at the short end of the market and this in turn is likely to influence the cost of finance for firms from debenture and preference shares or issues of new equity. Indeed, even if the firm uses retained profits to finance its real investment expenditure, changes in the market interest rates will still influence investment decisions. This is because one alternative to real investment is investment in marketable financial assets such as gilt-edged stock and other firms' equity. The higher the yield on the latter, the less likely it is that retained profits will be used by the firm to increase its own real investment expenditures.

Other influences

We have now discussed the main domestic factors that influence interest rates and we turn briefly to discuss influences that arise from the foreign sector, expectations and risk. It was argued in Chapter 7 that differences in foreign and domestic interest rates would reflect expectations of future changes in the exchange rate of foreign and domestic currencies (= uncovered interest rate parity). In practice, however, because future exchange-rate movements are uncertain and the UK resident may require a return on US assets that is higher than the known return on UK assets before he is willing to invest in the USA, there would need to be a risk premium before uncovered interest rate parity would apply.

In reality, there are many risks to investing in foreign assets. For example, there are institutional risks, on foreign bonds, such as risk of default, bankruptcy and the possible imposition of exchange controls. For investment in foreign equities or common stocks there is risk concerning the variability of returns on the foreign stock market, as well as risk due to movements of the exchange rate. This dampens international capital mobility but only to some extent.

Often the monetary authorities raise short-term interest rates to curtail excessive growth in domestic demand. The rise in domestic rates (if unanticipated) will attract a foreign capital inflow and put upward pressure on the exchange rate. In fact, as argued in Chapter 7, the exchange rate may initially overshoot its long-run value. It is the impact of an appreciation in the domestic currency on net trade and aggregate demand that often leads governments to abandon adherence to a tight monetary stance.

The uncovered interest rate parity (UIP) condition, together with a risk premium, provides a useful starting-point for the analysis of open economy factors that influence domestic interest rates. As an approximation, we may write 7.1 as:

$$r = r^* - u + \theta \tag{8.3}$$

where $u = \dfrac{S_{t+1}^e - S_t}{S_t}$ and θ is the risk premium. It is clear that foreign interest rates, r^*, are likely to influence domestic interest rates: a rise in US rates due, for example, to a tight monetary policy by the Federal Reserve Board will tend to lead to a capital outflow from the UK economy; bond prices in the UK fall and domestic interest rates rise, which tends to restore UIP. Note that with rational expectations a rise in domestic rates might occur at the time of the announcement of a tight US monetary policy, rather than when the actual money supply in the USA is cut.

A negative differential between UK and US interest rates can ensue (i.e. $r - r^* < 0$) if foreign-exchange speculators expect sterling to appreciate in the future (i.e. $\mu > 0$). An obvious factor here from the mid-1970s onwards was the discovery of North Sea oil and the rise in the world price of oil. These factors imply a strong UK oil balance in the future and FOREX dealers will expect sterling to appreciate. This may have allowed UK interest rates to fall relative to world interest rates in the 1980s.

Perceptions of risk can also drive a wedge between domestic and foreign interest rates. For example, even if FOREX dealers expect no change in the exchange rate ($\mu = 0$), UK interest rates may still be below US rates, ($r < r^*$), if speculators think the risk attached to their expectation of no change in the exchange rate has fallen (perhaps due to a firm credible commitment announced by the Government to maintain the existing exchange rate). While such market sentiment is difficult to quantify, it nevertheless impinges on UK interest rates, particularly in the short-term. If we broaden the UIP relationship so that it applies to uncertain capital assets (e.g. equities and long bonds), then r and r* are replaced by expected HPYs (on UK and US equities, say). In this case the expected HPY on UK equities may be below that on US equities because the former is perceived as less risky, perhaps because the variability in UK company profits, which directly influences the variability of UK equity prices, is perceived to be relatively small. To analyse this issue further requires use of the so-called international capital asset pricing model (CAPM) outlined in most introductory finance texts.

Like the exchange rate, day-to-day movements in interest rates are dominated by news or unanticipated events and this is what makes interest rates so volatile. Announcements about UK or foreign monetary and fiscal policy will be quickly assimilated by market-makers in the global money markets and reflected in new quoted interest rates. However, for most business decisions a longer-term view of interest-rate development is probably more important than these short-term movements due to news which may be quickly reversed.

Efficient markets?

The above discussion is largely based upon an 'efficient markets' view of the return on financial assets. This is that financial markets incorporate all the latest information about economic fundamentals. That seems hard to square with the extreme volatility of some financial markets. For example it is difficult to see what major changes in economic fundamentals (e.g.. forecast of dividends) could have occurred in the week of 19 October 1987 to cause the world's stock markets to crash by over 30 per cent. Evidence and new theoretical models are beginning to appear in the literature that suggest that herding behaviour could play a major role in determining fluctuations in financial markets in particular periods. One possibility is speculative bubble theory. In this case, investors get caught up in speculative bubbles for even though they realize that stocks are 'overvalued' in terms of fundamentals, they do not sell because they think someone will pay more for them tomorrow under the influence of mass psychology. When prices do begin to fall, they tumble. Keynes as usual neatly encapsulates the argument. Writing in 1936 he suggested that professional investors are concerned

> not with making superior long-term forecasts of the probable yield of an investment over its whole life but with foreseeing changes in the conventional basis of evaluation a short time ahead of the general public. They are concerned not with what an investment is worth to a man who buys it for keeps, but with what the market will value it at, under the influence of mass psychology, three months or a year hence. We have reached the third degree where we devote our intelligence to anticipating what average opinion expects average opinion to be.
>
> (Keynes, 1936, pp. 154-5)

Thus the winners are those who make their move fractionally ahead of everyone else.

An alternative explanation is catastrophe theory as outlined by Kettel (1989) and applied to equity markets. There are two groups of investors, fundamentalists and speculators. Fundamentalists start to buy when share prices are 'undervalued' whereas speculators wait until an upward price trend is established and then come in pushing up prices beyond equilibrium levels. After a while fundamentalists realize that stocks are overvalued and sell, followed eventually by the speculators who magnify the downward trend. Such volatility in certain financial markets may affect at least some interest rates.

8.4 INTEREST RATE FORECASTS

As noted above, movements in interest rates over the very short-term are not capable of being forecast as such movements are dominated by new information or news. In addition, very short-term *expectations* will influence day-to-day movements in interest rates. To give an example, it was widely expected that short-term UK interest rates would fall by at least half a per cent on budget day in April 1987. Market-makers, therefore, borrowed heavily in the overnight interbank market, pushing this borrowing rate up to around 35 per cent (at an annual rate). They used the proceeds to purchase (say) three-month commercial bills with a yield of about 9.5 per cent. On budget day, interest rates did fall by 0.5 per cent, that is, the market price of commercial bills rose. Market-makers then sold their bills, after holding them overnight, and used the capital gain to pay off the overnight interbank loan and make a profit on the deal. In this case, short-term expectations increased a key market rate, namely interbank rate, by a substantial amount. This behaviour is, in the main, unpredictable.

Over the medium and longer term (say three months to one year and one to five years respectively) we can obtain some insights into the future movements in interest rates. However, no forecast of interest rates can ever by anything more than an informed guess, even if this may be better than an uninformed one.

A useful starting-point is to consider what are the fundamental long-run forces affecting domestic UK interest rates. Uncovered interest parity indicates that the domestic interest rate, r, should equal the foreign interest rate, r^*, minus the expected appreciation in the domestic currency, μ, plus an adjustment for risk, θ:

$$r = r^* - \mu + \theta$$

What, then is likely to influence the expected appreciation or depreciation of the domestic currency in the long-run. Clearly the current account must balance in the longer term and broadly speaking, if long-run purchasing power parity applies, this requires the domestic inflation rate to equal the foreign rate. Hence in the long-run any forecast of interest rates must be based on:

1. Forecasts of foreign interest rates, r^*, especially US and German interest rates. These will be influenced by the monetary stance of the Federal Reserve Board and the Bundesbank. An overshoot in, say, US monetary targets can be expected to be followed by a rise in US rates and hence UK rates of interest.
2. Forecasts of relative inflation rates. The higher expected domestic inflation is or the faster inflation rises, then the greater the expected depreciation in sterling and the higher UK interest rates are likely to be.
3. The relative attractiveness of the domestic economy as reflected in the risk premium. This is difficult to quantify, but clearly perceived 'sound' government policies, the overall productivity of the economy and net inward direct investment by foreign companies are indicative of a 'strong' economy. In the case of the UK, increased North Sea oil output and the price of oil also reduce the perceived riskiness of investing in the UK relative to the US.

Over the medium term there are additional factors that need to be taken into account when forecasting interest rates. The most important of these is the policy stance of the Government. If the authorities have a monetary target, then any monetary growth in excess of the target range is likely to be met by a rise in interest rates by the Central Bank. For similar reasons, an overshoot in a PSBR target is also likely to result in the authorities financing this, in part, by future sales of government bonds, which will also raise interest rates.

Institutional changes can also impinge upon interest rates, particularly relative rates. Businesses have to keep a watchful eye on such developments as they directly impinge upon the cost of borrowing. These changes generally come under the heading of financial innovation. For example, in the UK in the early 1980s, after the introduction of more competition in the banking sector (i.e. competition and credit control) and among building societies post-1986, the interest differential between the borrowing rates and the lending rates in these institutions narrowed. In the case of the former, this attracted company treasurers to borrow relatively more via bank advances rather than directly on the stock exchange as well as to hold a high buffer stock of high-yielding liquid assets. Relaxation of credit controls on personal sector borrowing led to a substantial sharp rise in the debt–income ratio of people. Financial innovation and the ending of UK exchange controls in 1979 also led to a greater integration of domestic and overseas financial markets (for example, the Eurocurrency markets) and a plethora of new financial instruments (for example, floating rate notes, currency swaps, etc). This has meant that over the medium term the impact of foreign interest rates on domestic interest rates has been quicker and more potent. In forecasting, this implies that businesses may need to have a global view of developments in international capital markets if managers are to fully comprehend and attempt to forecast UK interest rates.

Questions

1. What do you understand by the term 'ripple effect'? Demonstrate how it would operate if the Government tried to increase the money supply by buying short-term commercial bills.
2. What is 'the term structure of interest rates'? How is it related to the 'yield' curve?
3. Why is the yield curve normally upward sloping? When might it be downward sloping?
4. What makes the yield curve shift downwards?
5. How would rational expectations on the part of speculators affect the response of interest rates to domestic and foreign government policy?
6. At 11 a.m. one day the Federal Reserve Board announces a target reduction in the growth of the US money supply of 5 per cent for the next financial year. UK interest rates immediately rise by 1 per cent. Later in the day, an announcement is made about the discovery of new oil reserves in the North Sea and the interest rate drops by 0.5 per cent. Explain why this might happen. If, on the other hand, UK interest rates remained stable after the rise in US rates, why might this happen?
7. 'The determination of interest rates is only partly explained by uncovered interest-rate parity.' Explain.
8. What is the efficient markets hypothesis? Does it apply in practice?
9. 'There are undoubtedly specific factors which affect financial markets in a non-random manner. The question is whether it is possible to take advantage of them to make excess returns.' Discuss.

8.5   RISK AVOIDANCE

Clearly, as with exchange rates it is unwise to rely on interest rate forecasts. This also means perhaps that it is unwise to put much faith in simple calculations of expected NPV and IRR values. Certainly it would be very sensible for a firm contemplating new investment to conduct sensitivity analysis using alternative interest rates and also alternative returns based on different assumptions about the general level of economic activity, rates of inflation, wage costs and so on. Again we seem to be back with the use of scenarios rather than specific forecast results.

It is perhaps not surprising in the context of the above discussions that so many UK firms use very simple methods of investment appraisal such as 'payback'. Such a crude approach may, however, give an undue weighting to the time value of risk and, therefore, an unreasonable bias towards short-term projects.

A more sensible approach both for individual businesses and the economy in general would be to utilize alternative sources of finance in terms of both types of funding and country of origin of funds. Company treasurers should be aware of the different costs of funds in different countries and may find it advantageous on occasion to enter into currency swaps with other companies in those countries which may be considered lower risk and, therefore, able to borrow at cheaper rates. These and related issues have been explored partially in the previous chapter. As far as domestic borrowing and lending are concerned, there is probably much to be said for the utilization of a balanced portfolio of funding including, of course, retained earnings. It may also be possible to lock into fixed interest rate borrowing for a specified period, though the company that takes out the loan 'loses' if interest rates subsequently fall. For this reason, some company treasurers prefer the variety of hedging strategies available. These include forward rate agreements, interest rate futures, and interest rate options.

With **forward rate agreements** (FRAs) borrowers agree an interest rate that they will pay in the future. Suppose a firm has a one-year floating rate loan which has to be rolled over every three months based on the three months interbank rate. For the first three months the rate will be fixed at the start of the contract. Assume, however, that the borrower thinks short-term interest rates will rise, so the cost of rolling over the loan three months from now will rise. He can hedge his risk by taking out an FRA for this next three-month period. At the start of the next quarter, he continues to borrow from his original lender. If the interbank interest rate is now greater than the rate agreed under the FRA contract then the *seller* of the contract will pay the *borrower* the difference. If on the other hand the interbank rate is lower, the borrower will compensate the seller. Either way the original borrower pays the net cost agreed under the FRA contract.

Interest rate futures are traded on exchanges and are standardized in terms of a set contract size, a specific settlement date and a specific interest period. Thus the person who buys an interest rate future has the right and obligation to deposit a sum of money for a specified interest rate for a specified period with the seller. The latter correspondingly takes on the right and obligation to take the deposit.

Such a future might be taken on by managers of a company needing to borrow in three months' time and expecting interest rates to rise. They would, therefore, sell an interest rate futures contract for delivery three months hence. The purchaser would be someone expecting interest rates to fall. Futures contracts for interest rates like other futures are registered with the relevant clearing house and there are compulsory initial and variation requirements for them all. They are mainly used by banks and financial institutions rather than corporate treasurers.

Interest rate options give the right but not the obligation to borrow or lend a sum of money at a fixed rate of interest for a fixed term at a specified future date in return for a premium. In this way, the purchaser of the option is protected against adverse interest rate movements but, unlike in the case of futures, the purchaser can also take advantage of any favourable movements by not exercising the option. Such options usually involve interest rate caps or floors. The seller of the cap compensates the purchaser if the cap rate is lower than some reference rate of interest such as the three month interbank rate. The buyer must pay a premium but benefits from the lower rate if the reference rate is lower than the cap by not exercising the option. Correspondingly an investor may purchase a floor below which he will be compensated by the seller if the reference rate falls below the floor. He or she will not exercise the option if the reference rate remains above the floor at the relevant time. Further details of these and other financial hedging strategies can be found in the excellent book by Buckley (1992).

Question

1. Explain the differences between forward rate agreements, interest rate futures and interest rate options.

8.6 CONCLUSION

In this chapter we have discussed the main sources and uses of funds within the domestic financial system. The huge flow of funds between financial institutions leads to the establishment of particular interest differentials or relative rates of return between different assets. These relative yields are influenced by the forces of supply and demand between the various markets and also by the actions of the monetary authorities.

The Central Bank can influence certain key interest rates by buying and selling assets (bills or long-term government bonds) in the market. This then has a ripple effect on other interest rates within the system and may lead to changes in the overall level of all interest rates, as well as changes in some interest differentials within the system. The authorities' impact on the absolute level of rates is far easier to predict than their impact on relative rates. Expectations, foreign interest rates and perceptions of risk can also have a major impact on domestic interest rates. Perhaps the most important linkage is between UK and US and German short-term interest rates: unless exchange-rate expectations alter, changes in these interest rates have a very strong impact on UK rates. Largely extraneous factors (for example, oil price rises) can also affect UK interest rates as they alter foreigners' perceptions of the general level of risk in investing in UK companies (the 'strong economy factor') or FOREX dealers' views about the expected change in the exchange rate. Both these effects work via the uncovered interest parity relationship.

The reader must obviously be aware of the high degree of volatility in financial markets as interest rates, bond and equity prices, and exchange rates can undergo very substantial changes over short periods. One question that arises is whether such movements are the result of actions by rational agents based on economic fundamentals or whether they are heavily influenced by whim, caprice and general expectations.

At present this appears to be an open question. Evidence and new theoretical models are beginning to appear in the literature that suggest that herding behaviour could play a major role in determining fluctuations in financial markets in particular periods. If correct, and stock prices are not based on economic fundamentals, then there is a possible rationale for government intervention in the market. The latter has always been a hotly debated issue in the market for foreign exchange where governments have over substantial periods tried to influence the exchange rate (e.g. the Plaza and Louvre Agreements of the late 1980s on stablizing exchange rates of the major industrialized (G7) countries and the setting up of the ERM). Also, as we have seen, governments do not usually leave the movement of interest rates solely to market forces, but intervene via active open market operations.

Thus if asset prices such as interest rates and exchange rates left solely to market forces produce excess volatility and undesirable macroeconomic effects, the authorities may damp down such movements by announcing bands and target ranges for these variables. This does not necessarily mean that they will be successful at achieving them.

To repeat, the importance of the future course of interest rates is of obvious importance for the solvency and future investment plans of individual firms. In this chapter we hope we have dealt with the main macroeconomic forces, that impinge upon interest rates (and other asset prices) so that the businessman can analyse the material in the financial press and on government policy, and can adopt appropriate responses.

9 The role of policy

> There is no art which one government sooner learns than that of draining money from the pockets of the people.
>
> (Adam Smith)

In previous chapters, frequent mention has been made of policy as an important influence on the financial and international environments, and in the determination of prices and output levels. It therefore seems appropriate to examine the role of policy in some detail, for policy decisions will greatly affect individual businesses. Business persons will, therefore, wish to be aware of the main policy controversies, particularly as the policy arena is perhaps the one important area where they can, through various channels, affect the policy formulation process. In the UK the various channels include, of course, the political parties, the Confederation of British Industry, the Institute of Directors, the National Economic Development Office and the professional organizations representing particular industries and/or skills. Other countries have similar bodies.

In assessing the role of policy it is important to bear in mind the policy aims. Sometimes these may conflict with one another as, for example, in the case of low unemployment and low inflation, or they may differ in the short and long-run. An individual government may, for example, be more interested in winning an election at a certain time than in worrying about the long-term performance of the economy should it get re-elected. It follows, therefore, that we need to decide on a standard by which business persons would want to judge economic policy at the macroeconomic level. A 'healthy economy' would be a reasonable criterion as evidenced by a high and consistent rate of output growth, low inflation and low unemployment. (Many would also argue for a high-quality physical environment, which they might not want to be compromised by the growth of GDP as currently measured.)

In what follows, we begin with a wide perspective in examining the general case for intervention versus non-intervention before turning to detailed consideration of different levels of intervention and different types of interventionist approach. We then examine some particular policy issues of relevance in the late 1990s.

9.1 INTERVENTION VERSUS NON-INTERVENTION

The debate on the extent to which governments should interfere in the running of economies was revived as recession in the 1970s became partly identified with excessive intervention in many developed countries. The result was a significant shift to the right and in many countries an increased reliance on market forces. It must be stressed that we are only talking in relative terms, for all governments need to interfere to some extent in providing, for example, defence and central banking. Moreover, governments are constrained by the fact that, in practice, most developed economies have a substantial public sector reflecting a less than complete reliance on the market mechanism. The argument is, then, whether economic prosperity is better achieved by decreasing or increasing government involvement.

The case for decreasing involvement is based on the views of the classical economists. Their views were founded on the doctrine of *laissez-faire* and they believed that the process of competition would serve society best. Market forces would ensure that only those business persons who correctly anticipated the wants of consumers at a point in time would make profits, these being regarded as a desirable reward for enterprise. Given changes in preferences, changes in technology and continued competition, there was no need for government intervention. It was not needed to curb the excesses of the market, such as monopoly profits, because competition would ensure that they did not last and it was not needed to pump-prime an economy as businesses would be better able than government to take both a long- and a short-term view of profit-making opportunities. Finally, it was not needed to improve wage levels because wage levels above those set by supply and demand in the labour market would mean higher unemployment. The labour force would be best served in the long-run by a flexible unregulated economy.

The classical view of competition as a process has been revived, in the last twenty years, with the increasing influence of Austrian economists such as Hayek. Such classicists argue that less government intervention and a return to *laissez-faire* are necessary to solve the fundamental weaknesses of western industry. The basis of their beliefs is that business persons know best and in exercising their own self-interest they will be maximizing the welfare of society.

Monetarist and particularly new-classical ideas are clearly in the classic tradition. In the monetarist case, the argument is that intervention should be limited to the keeping of simple rules of the type that the growth of the money supply should be pre-announced and based upon the Government's inflation target. Monetarists argue against the Keynesian view that monetary and fiscal policy can be used to increase the stability of the business environment by smoothing out the booms and slumps that are otherwise endemic to the capitalist system. Indeed, monetarists argue that demand management may, in fact, be destabilizing with regard to the trade cycle. By the time the Government has realized that the economy has gone into recession and has intervened to correct it, the economy would in all probability already be recovering. Thus government intervention would be likely to amplify the cycle by giving an added boost to the economy when it did not need it.

The stop-go era of the 1950s and 1960s and the Lawson boom of the late 1980s in the UK suggest some support for this view.

New-classical economists go even further by arguing that only unanticipated policy changes will have any impact, albeit a temporary one, on the real economy. However, such unanticipated changes should be avoided, as they tend to increase the variability of output while leaving the overall level of rate of growth unaffected.

Such ideas have gained widespread support in recent years in a number of developed countries ranging from the particularly free market of the USA, to the traditionally more interventionist European countries and Japan. They have led to the adoption of monetarist policies on the demand side of the economy while on the supply-side encouragement has been given to privatization, to the abandonment of 'lame ducks' and to the promotion of new and small firms. Supply-side policies of this type have not just been adopted by individual European governments; they have also been increasingly espoused by the European Union.

While the adoption of such policies may have revived some firms and even revitalized some economies, there is little evidence that they are a universal panacea. As far as the demand side of economic policy has been concerned, control of the money supply seems to have been a particularly illusive policy instrument – the 'uncontrollable in pursuit of the indefinable' as one UK commentator caustically put it (Gilmour, 1983, p. 142). It now seems to have been effectively abandoned in the UK, in particular, as the sole indicator of the thrust of monetary policy. Even on the supply-side, the policies may not have worked as intended in the UK, for example, there was a significant narrowing of the productivity gap in manufacturing relative to competitor countries between 1979 and 1993 but the main reason for this was the setting up in the UK of Japanese, German, American and other foreign-owned plants rather than the direct result of the development of an enterprise culture (Eltis, 1995). These foreign-owned plants have introduced quality control techniques and a managerial style which has spread widely to British-owned companies.

In any event, evidence from a variety of developed countries would suggest that the unfettered free market does not provide the only solution to economic growth. Details of economic growth are given in Table 9.1 for a number of developed countries over the long-term.

The fastest growing country of those listed has been Japan, where there has been close co-operation and planning between government and big business even though as in America the State contribution to GDP has been relatively low for highly developed countries. Similarly, indicative planning operated in France, and in Germany there has been close co-operation between banks and industry. Even in the USA, the bastion of free enterprise, much of the success of the whole economy and certainly of areas within it over certain time periods has been largely influenced by government defence procurement.

We should be wary of overcriticizing the classical case, however. There are cases where markets do not provide an optimal solution (for example, innovation and training) and also cases where the self-interest of the business person does not square with the interests of the economy (for example, insider

Table 9.1 Growth of real gross domestic product

	Average year-to-year percentage changes		
	1968–73	*1973–9*	*1979–94*
USA	3.2	2.4	2.3
Japan	8.7	3.6	3.5
Germany	4.9	2.3	2.3
France	5.4	2.8	2.0
UK	3.4	1.5	2.0
Italy	4.5	3.7	2.2
Canada	5.4	4.2	2.5

Source: Organization for Economic Co-operation and Development

dealing). Equally, there are cases where public intervention (for example, some nationalization) has not been a great success and where increased competition has benefited the consumer. Moreover, there is an issue of the sustainability of interventionist programmes in areas such as welfare in the highly competitive global market conditions of the late 1990s. One source of that competition is the so called Asian tiger economies, which invest heavily in education and training but have low public spending particularly on welfare. Even within the EU, however, countries such as Germany are finding it increasingly difficult to compete with lower labour cost countries such as the UK with the result that some German firms are relocating production to those lower-cost countries. Moreover, in Japan it appears that the job for life ethic in large enterprises can no longer be sustained.

Either way, turning to the interventionist case, there are good and bad examples of policy. In most countries there has been a great deal of intervention to support declining industries, to support declining areas, to develop the wrong industries and to disguise unemployment. All this suggests that it is not so much intervention versus non-intervention that should be the main issue but rather, perhaps, where to intervene and how to formulate good as opposed to bad policy to complement the basic market system.

Questions

1. To what extent should governments intervene in the running of an economy?
2. Consider the extent to which the performance of the UK economy benefited from Thatcherism.
3. 'Privatization in the UK has done little more than substitute private for public monopoly.' Discuss.
4. 'The argument should not be about intervention or non-intervention. It should be about good or bad policy.' Discuss.
5. A financier, an industrialist and a right-wing politician meet to discuss future direction of economic policy. How do you think the discussion might go?

Box 9.1 Cutting back the role of the State

The State has gradually become highly influential in all modern societies though, as Table 9.2 shows, there are big differences between various countries. Of those listed France and Italy currently have more than half of GDP resulting from government expenditure, a far higher proportion than in the US and Japan where a figure of just over a third applies.

Table 9.2 Government expenditure as a percentage of gross domestic product.

	c.1870	c.1913	c.1937	1960	1994
UK	9.4	12.7	30.0	32.2	42.9
USA	3.9	1.8	8.6	27.0	33.5
Germany	10.0	14.8	42.4	32.4	49.0
France	12.6	17.0	29.0	34.6	54.9
Italy	11.9	11.1	24.5	30.1	53.9
Japan	8.8	8.3	25.4	17.5	35.8
Singapore	n.a	n.a	n.a	n.a	19.0

In the economies of the 'Asian tigers' such as Singapore, the level of government activity is a great deal smaller.

Right-wing economists and politicians argue that the extent of government activity is now too high and that public spending must be drastically reduced if 'Western' economies are to remain competitive. In the UK, for example, Conservative politicians aim to reduce state activity to less than 40 per cent of GDP.

The evidence of Tanzi and Schuknecht (1995) suggests that the expansion of state activity from 1870 to 1960 brought considerable benefits in terms of social advances with lower unemployment, lower infant mortality and general death rates, better schooling and a more equal distribution of income. It also suggests that there are sharply diminishing returns to state activity once it has absorbed more than 20–30 per cent of national income. Surprisingly, for example, countries with relatively large government sectors seem to allocate only marginally more income to the poorest 40 per cent of their population compared to those with small government sectors. The authors conclude that large government sectors result in a large 'black' economy, a higher unemployment rate and a lower rate of private sector innovation because of the higher marginal tax rates required to finance them.

As Davies (1996) has argued, an alternative hypothesis is that economies which perform badly for quite different reasons may generate demands for extra social security and public services so that causation is reversed.

Either way, reducing the role of the State is far from easy. One problem is state pensions, which have increased greatly in importance with the larger percentage of old people and falling retirement age. It is hard to reduce current pensions because current pensioners cannot go out to work to supplement their income. It is also hard to hit current workers who are paying for the present pensions and look forward to receiving them too in due course. Moreover, consumers are demanding even higher standards of health care and education and expect the State to provide it. Finally, unemployment seems to be on a long-term upward trend as technological progress reduces labour requirements not just in manufacturing, but also in services. Redistribution from those in work to those without it may, therefore, be increasingly necessary to maintain the fabric of society.

9.2 TYPES OF POLICY

Policies may broadly be split into those primarily affecting the supply-side of an economy and those affecting the demand side.

Supply-side policies, which have become increasingly popular, include privatization and deregulation. Evidence for the UK suggests that, in many cases, efficiency has improved as a result. There is some doubt, however, as to whether the full gains have gone to the consumer for, in many cases, to make sell-offs attractive to investors, monopoly positions have been maintained, at least for a particular time, while the regulatory framework has been weak.

Longer-standing supply-side policies of the interventionist type have included tripartite planning agreements between industry, trade unions and government, as operated for many years in Scandinavia, Japan and France. The idea here is that economic growth is better fostered by an atmosphere of collaboration than confrontation, and it certainly did seem to be successful for long periods in the above cases. Other supply-side policies include subsidies and grants to particular industries.

In recent years, all governments have seen the need to promote the growth of micro-electronics, for example, and none has been prepared to leave this completely to market forces. Whether they should have done so or, alternatively, intervened to a greater extent is of some interest given long-standing problems in European micro-electronics.

Also in recent years, many grants and allowances have been directed at new entrepreneurs and existing small firms, and at training and retraining and, in the UK, these policies undoubtedly contributed to the net growth in businesses from 1.9 million in 1979 to 2.8 million in 1993. Yet other policies have been directed at particularly underdeveloped, depressed or developing areas, such as the regional policy of the EU and various member states. A key supply-side policy in some countries is tax cuts for individuals and firms, the idea being to encourage an enterprise culture, innovation and productivity.

A final supply-side measure is incomes policy. The idea here, as argued in Chapter 3 is to enable demand-side policies to ensure an appropriate supply-side response. Although new incomes policies of the tax-based variety are still advocated in some quarters (Layard, 1986), past policies do not appear to have been very successful in the UK – except in the short-run.

This brings us to the demand side and in particular, to monetary and fiscal policy, which we have already examined in some detail. It might be argued that demand-side policy of some kind is necessary to provide an environment conducive to business optimism. Keynesians, in particular, would argue that although supply-side considerations are important they are not on their own sufficient to encourage business persons to undertake investment in a period of recession. An example is provided by wage cuts, given that these are frequently suggested by monetarists as a cure to unemployment. But wage cuts on their own are likely to depress aggregate demand and why should firms take on more labour or, indeed, expand output when sales are falling? All this suggests that demand considerations do not and should not operate independently of supply. As for which type of demand-side policy, there are, as suggested above, interdependencies between monetary and fiscal policy, and in the USA the Reagan administration used both simultaneously. Indeed, perhaps more controversy is attached to which type of fiscal or monetary policy. As far as monetary policy is concerned, there has been little success in controlling the broad monetary aggregates and reliance is now back on a 'look at everything' approach in the monetary field.

As far as fiscal policy is concerned there is the question of whether increased public expenditure or tax cuts are the best method of controlling an economy. Assume we wish to expand the economy by fiscal means. Those in favour of tax cuts stress that the individual should decide where to spend his or her money and that incentive effects are important, while those in favour of public expenditure argue that much of the benefit of tax cuts in highly open economies such as the UK is likely to leak into imports. Thus tax cuts have both a supply-side (i.e. incentive effect) and a demand-side effect. Just how effective they are is open to doubt certainly as regards the UK for despite headline cuts in rates of income tax, the total tax take has gone up since 1979. Tax thresholds and indirect taxes such as VAT (value added tax) have gone up with the result that the rich have gained at the expense of the poor. The latter category, which has expanded, have tended to be stuck in a benefits trap with little incentive to find work. Thus Conservative policies have been blamed for a rise in dependency (Parker, 1995).

Other possible demand-side measures include the restriction of imports and the encouragement of exports, although risks of retaliation can be significant and there is now a general trend to removing import restrictions via the GATT (General Agreement on Tariffs and Trade) negotiations, the opening up of Eastern Europe and the removal of trade barriers within the EU.

Having looked at policy in general, we now turn to some specific policy issues of the moment, the first of which is whether the UK should embrace a single currency.

Questions

1. Distinguish between demand- and supply-side interventionist policies. Give examples of each.
2. Why are tax cuts both a demand- and supply-side policy? Would this also apply to investment?
3. 'In practice it is not easy to distinguish the supply- and demand-side of the economy and they are certainly not independent of one another.' Discuss.

4. Evaluate the success of supply-side industrial policy as applied to training and/or innovation in any one country by comparing it with others.
5. 'Britain's economic problem has been too many scarce resources directed at defence.' Discuss.
6. 'The peace-dividend will bring benefits to all parts of the UK.' Discuss.

9.3 THE CASE FOR A EUROPEAN SINGLE CURRENCY

This remains a highly contentious issue in the UK, though it is far less of an issue in continental Europe, where it is regarded as a further building block in the creation of a united, single market Europe. The advantage of a single currency is that it saves on transactions costs of doing business across national frontiers. Financial costs of changing money will no longer exist and there will be savings in the time, effort and resources involved in monitoring movements in individual EU currencies when determining financial portfolio, pricing and real investment decisions. (The European Commission has estimated financial cost savings from adopting a common currency at about 1.5 per cent of EU GDP.) With a single currency, member states effectively enter a monetary 'United States of Europe', with a 'Eurofed' Central Bank, which sets the single Euro interest rate, payable in terms of the single currency. Thus the UK would become much like the state of Texas in the USA, namely a region of this new common currency area.

If one is a monetarist, then the inflation rate throughout the whole EU will be set by the monetary policy of the Eurofed, and monetary sovereignty of the UK Bank of England is lost. Interest-rate changes and hence any impact upon the UK domestic economy are determined by the Eurofed, not by the Bank of England and the UK Chancellor. Clearly sovereignty over monetary policy is pooled in the constitutional set-up of the Eurofed – which is, at present, unknown (e.g. a simple example would be where each Central Banker has one vote and majority voting applies to all decisions). We have noted that interest rates do have an impact on the real economy and hence on unemployment, and the UK government will have no immediate direct control over this Euro interest rate.

Clearly, with a common currency one also loses the ability to devalue and improve ones' competitive position (e.g. Texas cannot devalue relative to Oklahoma in the US). However, it is arguable that devaluation only gives a very short-lived competitive advantage, as higher import prices lead to a domestic wage–price spiral and any initial competitive advantage is quickly eroded, say, over three years.

Fiscal policy (i.e. change in government expenditures, unemployment benefits and tax rates) in principle remains a viable option for individual member states to influence aggregate demand and unemployment (e.g. the State of Texas has its own budgetary powers). However, individual states may have to be constrained in their fiscal stance over a run of years. Individual Euro-states in the common currency area cannot finance their fiscal deficits by printing money as this is to be determined by the Eurofed and must, therefore, sell their own bonds (e.g. the State of New York issues its own bonds to finance additional spending). The interest rate on the bonds will, of course be in terms of the single currency. However, interest rates on the bonds of profligate states may be higher than in states that adopt a prudent fiscal policy, in order to reflect the higher possible default risk. Even so, a relatively large element of fiscal autonomy could remain with individual countries even under a single currency.

It is widely anticipated that the effect of the single market will be to reinforce the core at the expense of the periphery. If regional problems arise as a result in the UK or in one of its regions or indeed elsewhere in Europe, then the only options are labour or firm 'migration' or fiscal transfers. Unlike the USA, language problems will hinder labour migration from high to low unemployment countries. Nationalistic tensions could arise in areas of high unemployment where some 'immigrant workers' have jobs. An alternative to workers moving to the work is firms moving to the (unemployed) workers. To some extent this should happen if real wage costs are low and other economic conditions, including transport links and other infrastructure, are favourable in the high unemployment area. It should be noted that many UK and European regional disparities are very long standing so we cannot be confident that adjustment to market differentials will occur over anything but a long time horizon. Though the increased resources devoted to European regional policy should help, the funds are very limited compared to the problems faced.

This all rather suggests that a single currency will benefit the strong rather than the weak. It may be that only the strong will be invited to join, for the Maastricht summit of December 1991 laid down strict convergence criteria. These were as follows:

1. *Price stability*: no country participating in the common currency should have an inflation rate greater than 1.5 per cent above the average of the three EU countries with the lowest price rises.
2. *Interest rates*: a similar convergence criterion applies to long-term interest rates, but the band this time is no more than two per centage points above the average of the three lowest interest rates.
3. *Fiscal deficits*: national budget deficits must be less than 3 per cent of GDP.
4. *Public debt*: the ratio of the stock of outstanding public debt (for example, primarily outstanding Treasury bills and gilt-edged stock in the UK) must not exceed 60 per cent of GDP.
5. *Currency stability*: a national currency must have been within the normal 2.25 per cent fluctuation margins of the ERM and must not have been devalued in the previous two years, in the run-up to the common currency period. (Given the widening of the bands following the problems with the ERM this no longer appears valid.)

The UK secured a binding protocol at Maastricht which allows it to decide whether to opt out of the common currency even if it meets the criteria. As we have seen, the UK government would then lose the ability to devalue and to set interest rates. Just how much of a loss these are, is open to doubt. Certainly, devaluation greatly increased UK competitiveness and exports following withdrawal from the ERM in 1992, but it could be argued that the pound had entered the ERM at too high a rate of exchange in the first place. Moreover, the benefits of devaluation are rarely long lasting. As for interest rates, the possibilities for divergence from those of other industrialized countries are limited. Finally, those that argue strongly for keeping the UK policy options open by not joining in should perhaps examine just how well those options have been exercised in the past.

Opting in would increase the influence of the UK in Brussels, would offer better possibilities for cross-border investment and sales by British firms, would help maintain the attractiveness of the UK economy to inward investment from countries such as the USA and Japan, and might maintain London's importance as a financial centre relative to say Frankfurt. There would, however, be likely to be regional problems arising from entry and the difficulty here is that the UK is unlikely to receive large sums from what is a small regional budget. The reasons are that UK regional disparities are small relative to those in other countries and that the problems of even the worst-performing UK regions pale into insignificance with those in the poor southern parts of the EU.

Perhaps the worst scenario for the UK and for UK businesses is that Britain will be left behind in a two-tier Europe by those countries which do meet the convergence criteria and which do enthusiastically embrace both the single currency and the European ideal.

We now turn to another contentious issue referred to in the single currency debate, regional policy.

Questions

1. Consider whether a single European currency is likely to be:
   (a) feasible
   (b) good for Europe
   (c) good for the UK.
2. 'It will be better for business if there is complete monetary union within the European Union.' Discuss.
3. 'The problem with the EMS was that it was a halfway house.' Discuss.
4. 'If the single currency fails to materialize, many peripheral regions in the UK and elsewhere will be rejoicing.' Discuss.

9.4 THE CASE FOR REGIONAL POLICY

As argued above, this is considered essential by the European Union. Traditional regional policy directed at backward or declining regions may be justified on a variety of economic grounds. The first as argued above, is that peripheral regions of the EU may lose out as the pull of the core increases with the single market. This could apply for a number of reasons. One is that central regions are closest to the main population centres, a positioning which may give scale economies. A second is that since central regions contain the main urban centres, they have the best transport and telecommunications facilities. A third is that since the main urban centres are important financial and administrative locations, firms in or near them have easy access to financial resources and political clout. A fourth is that central regions may have grown at the expense of the periphery sucking in the best labour and capital. Finally, peripheral regions tend to have a high per centage of small firms which are uncompetitive with multinationals which tend to be located in the core. To bring everyone on board it is essential to offer help directed at the periphery.

A second justification for regional policy voiced over the long-term in the UK is that centralizing economic activity in the core will lead to migration and the waste of social capital (i.e. schools and hospitals) in peripheral and declining areas and the duplication of such capital in the core. This argument has usually been invalidated by general population growth, though a stagnating European population may give it some relevance in the future.

A third argument for regional policy is that the expansion of the core will impose congestion costs on firms which need to be encouraged to move to alternative destinations on the assumptions that market forces will take too long to operate.

A fourth long-standing argument is that the European growth rate will increase if the labour reserves of the peripheral and depressed areas are utilized. This hardly seems relevant in the context of very high actual or concealed unemployment throughout the EU.

A final argument, perhaps more relevant in the case of individual nations, is that unbalanced growth may add to inflationary pressures. Thus fast growth in say the South-East of England may bid up wages which would be transmitted by national wage agreements across the country giving a boost to national inflation.

For any or all of these reasons, interventionists have traditionally argued for regional policy directed at problem regions and that is the present focus of regional policy at both European and individual country level. Thus, the European Commission directs policy at three groups of areas. The first is Objective 1 regions which have 79 per cent or less of EU GDP per capita. Over 80 per cent of EU regional funds are allocated to such regions, only three of which are in the UK (Merseyside, Northern Ireland, Highlands and Islands). The second is Objective 2 regions which are those in industrial decline. There are many of these regions in the UK such as parts of the North-East and of South Wales. The third is Objective 5b which are lagging rural regions (e.g. much of Devon and Cornwall) not covered by Objective 1.

It is interesting to examine how such regional policy fits with the free market–interventionist debate above. Those on the right tend to argue that regional problems are best covered by improving the operation of market forces by, for example, scrapping national wage bargaining, minimum wages or general social security provision. Traditional interventionists suggest that market forces have done very little to alleviate long-standing regional differentials and must be supplemented by enormous government transfers of money from rich to poor regions.

It is also reasonable to take a different interventionist stand to reinforce rather than hamper market tendencies. This may be examined from a UK perspective in a European context. UK regional policy has invariably been directed at taking work to the workers from the prosperous South-East to the declining industrial areas of Scotland, Northern Ireland, Wales, the North of England and, latterly, the far South-West and also offering aid to foreign inward investors to locate in the latter destinations. This is all well and good if a rich, capacity-constrained South-East can export its surplus industry to the periphery. But what if the UK as a whole is considered a backward region of Europe and, within the UK, the South-East is only relatively rich in a UK sense and far from capacity-constrained? Might it not be argued that, in such circumstances, the best thing the UK can do is to concentrate resources in the areas of greatest economic potential, including the South-East. Thus, instead of subsidizing problem regions, it might be argued that the subsidy should be concentrated on say high technology industry and the infrastructure to support it in the M4 corridor west of Heathrow. In this way, the UK will benefit whereas traditional policy would simply result in further draining a half-empty reservoir. The same arguments could equally apply to Europe in total trying to maximize its competitive position in a world trading system.

These two policy examples, therefore, illustrate the potential role of alternative policy stances ranging from freeing up markets to alternative forms of intervention. Other topics which might usefully be examined are education and training, research and development, and transport infrastructure where there are big differences between different EU member states. These are not considered here but can easily be explored in the literature.

Questions

1. Evaluate the economic case for regional policy in a) Europe, and b) the UK. What form should any such policy take?
2. 'The UK will be unlikely to get much help from Europe for its regional problems and it will not be able to do much about them itself.' Discuss.
3. Examine the economic arguments for a regional policy aimed at improving the economic prospects of the most prosperous parts of the UK.
4. 'Traditional regional policy has been completely unsuccessful in the UK.' Discuss.
5. What is the 'additionality' problem?
6. 'There are great regional disparities in the EU and within individual EU countries, and there is little indication that things are improving.' Discuss.

9.5 SUMMARY

This chapter has outlined the various controversies regarding the role of economic policy and it would be possible to write a book on these issues alone. Business persons will clearly have their own views on which type of policy is most appropriate both for a trading bloc or country generally, and for their industry/firms in particular. We hope, however, that this book has helped them to formulate an informed position and that, therefore, they will be effective in making their voices heard both within their own firms and in the wider public domain.

Overview 10

We have now concluded our examination of the major macroeconomic influences affecting business. We finish by drawing together some of the important points made in previous chapters.

We begin by restating that the business environment is constantly changing and firms must adapt to survive. At one time the theoretical literature of both micro and industrial economics was largely about firms reacting passively to the environment and particularly the market structure which they faced. It is now increasingly recognized that successful firms engage in *active* behaviour both to understand and to mould that environment. To do so they require a strategy to reduce the level of uncertainty, to maximize their responsiveness to change and to achieve the targets they set themselves. This applies in the long-run, an area which is normally covered by courses in business policy, and also to short-run decisions in the so-called functional areas of finance, marketing, production and the management of labour resources. It is, therefore, clearly important that both business persons and business students understand the importance of the operating environment and the effect it can have on business decisions.

There are many influences which affect business and we have focused on the macroeconomic ones. In doing so, we have attempted in most cases to lay down general principles which can be applied across a wide spectrum of business rather than to present a case study approach. The reason is that every business is unique and so are many business problems. We can only hope that the reader is now better equipped to understand the importance of changes in the macroeconomy and how to allow for them.

Our first point concerns inflation and its effect on the planning of budgets. Inflation affects the costs of goods and labour, and also future selling prices, so it is extremely important that business persons allow for it in both the planning process and the negotiation of contracts. We have, therefore, examined in some detail both the theoretical determinants of price changes and also inflation forecasts.

The second point we have emphasized is that business persons should be aware of the information available on the macroeconomy and should be able both to use and interpret it. This applies both to past and present data and to the use of forecasts. As we argued in Chapter 6, this can be done with various degrees of sophistication and the day is fast approaching when business persons can produce their own forecasts on personal computers or conduct sensitivity analyses on somebody else's macroeconomic model at relatively low cost. Though it is easy to exaggerate the usefulness of economic forecasts, they do allow the consideration of alternative scenarios allowing for feedback effects.

The third point is that business persons need to be aware of the international aspects of business, particularly if they operate in an economy as open as that of the UK. We have examined issues such as the use of hedging, portfolio diversification, and the forward market to avoid exchange rate risk. We have also looked at longer-term measures for diversifying foreign assets such as the establishment of foreign subsidiaries. These are important aspects of modern business.

An interesting example of a firm which partly failed because of exchange rate factors was Laker Airways which folded in 1982. Although recession in the airline industry, high interest rates and a very high debt to equity ratio were also important, Laker's problems were compounded by the fact that some of the borrowing was in the USA and had to be repaid in dollars. The weakening of the sterling-dollar exchange rate and the fact that much of the firm's income was presumably in sterling 'wreaked havoc' with its 1981–2 budget (Donne and Friedman, 1982). The Laker case demonstrates the interaction between exchange rates and capital markets, a topic which we have examined in some detail. Clearly business persons need to be aware of the importance of international interest rates and of the financial policies of domestic and foreign governments (see Box 10.1 for another example).

The fourth point, then, concerns awareness and relates to both international and domestic capital markets. One aspect of this is that the cost of capital to a firm depends on the mix of finance chosen which, in turn, depends on a whole set of interest rates, from those on bank loans to those on bonds and equity. Foreign rates also play a part as firms increasingly seek funds in Euromarkets. The possible adoption of a single European currency will considerably alter the market environment faced by business in Europe, whoever signs up for it in the first instance.

It is, of course, important for firms to diversify their domestic as well as their foreign assets. The case of London and Counties Securities is illustrative in this respect. This secondary bank borrowed money on the London money markets which it then invested very largely in 'illiquid' property during the property boom of the early 1970s. The problem was that the company borrowed 'short' and lent 'long' so that, when short-term interest rates rose, its profits were squeezed. In addition, the end of the property boom made its assets less valuable and depositors began to lose confidence. There was a run on deposits and the Bank of England had to step in to rescue the bank and to prevent a crisis of confidence in the banking system as a whole. Unfortunately, the lessons were not entirely learnt. The 'boom' in the 1980s led to extensive property speculation in many parts of the developed world. The onset of recession at the end of the decade caused a slump in property values and many property companies in the UK in particular went bankrupt. As a result bank profits fell significantly and so did bank lending dampening investment and increasing company liquidations in the wider economy.

Our final point is that business persons need to know how policy changes

Box 10.1 Brittany Ferries

The case of Brittany Ferries illustrates many of the economic and political influences affecting businesses discussed in previous chapters. Originally set up in Brittany to transport agricultural produce to the UK via Plymouth, the company has become an important operator on the long Channel crossing routes from Cork, Plymouth, Poole and Portsmouth to Roscoff, Cherbourg, St Malo and Caen. The company also runs a service to Santander in Northern Spain from Plymouth in the summer months and from Portsmouth in the winter. On all these routes, it is the major competitor to P & O which operates out of Portsmouth and Southampton to Cherbourg and to Bilbao.

Both companies have been badly affected by falling demand in the 1990s as English holiday-makers have been put off travelling to France by the much higher cost of living there resulting from the 'franc fort' policy and the withdrawal of the UK from the ERM. However, Brittany Ferries has faced particular problems because most of its earnings are in sterling while its costs must be paid in francs. Moreover, as the company uses French crews it has to pay for the much higher social benefits which French workers receive. Indeed, Brittany Ferries has a welfare and benefits bill costing £10m per annum more than that of P & O. All French sea captains, for example, retire at 55, ten years earlier than their British counterparts (*Sunday Times*, 1996). In total French labour costs are 30 per cent higher than those of their British counterparts, so that firms such as Brittany Ferries have a major competitive disadvantage. One obvious possibility would be to move operations to the British ports and to use British crews. Another would be to try to increase the number of French relative to British travellers.

On a wider scale, cases such as this question the countinuance of the British opt-out from the social contract and indeed whether floating currencies within Europe can continue to be acceptable in a true single market.

No doubt 'exceptional' subsidies will continue to ameliorate competitive pressures; in the spring of 1996, Brittany Ferries was asking for tax breaks from the French government to 'tide it over'.

are likely to affect them. In the short-run, we have emphasized that this is a matter of how best to adapt to policy announcements given their likely impact on the major economic variables such as exchange rates, interest rates and wages and prices. In the long-run, it is a question of how business persons can understand and contribute to the debates essential to the formulation of policies affecting the economic environment in which they operate.

Glossary

C	=	consumer's expenditure (real)
CB	=	current account balance
D	=	dividend
F	=	forward exchange rate
G	=	government expenditure
I	=	investment expenditure (real)
M	=	imports or money supply (sometimes M_S)
MC	=	marginal cost
MR	=	marginal revenue
M_D	=	money demand
m	=	rate of growth of money supply (percentage)
P	=	aggregate price level (domestic) (except in section 8.3)
P*	=	aggregate price level (foreign)
p	=	domestic rate of growth of price level (inflation) (percentage)
p*	=	foreign rate of inflation
R	=	yield to maturity on a bond
r	=	interest rate (domestic)
r*	=	interest rate (foreign)
S	=	spot exchange rate
s	=	percentage change in the exchange rate
T	=	tax (except in section 2.1)
U	=	actual unemployment (percentage)
U_0	=	natural rate of umempolyment or NAIRU
V	=	velocity of circulation
W	=	level of nominal wages
w	=	rate of wage inflation
X	=	exports
Y	=	level of real output (GDP) or income
Y_0	=	natural rate of output
y	=	growth of real income (percentage)
θ	=	risk premium
μ	=	expected appreciation of the home currency

superscript 'e' indicates expected value of a variable

Further reading

Below we give a highly selective list of further reading on the topics covered in this text. Except where stated otherwise the references listed should provide a manageable increase in the degree of complexity of exposition.

CHAPTERS 2, 3 AND 4

There is a plethora of introductory macroeconomics texts including Begg *et al.* (1991), which provides a nice balance between theory and recent historical narrative for the UK. A very useful short foundation book is available in Blake (1993). Dornbusch and Fischer (1990) use primarily US examples. Crystal (1983) and Pratten (1990) also provide a succinct account and link theory with 'real world' models of the UK economy, while Artis (1984) provides a useful, concise development of the main theoretical issues. Another useful applied reference for the UK is Griffiths and Wall (1995).

CHAPTER 5

Davis and Pointon (1994) and Lumby (1984) provide a clear, thorough introduction to investment appraisal, other financial decisions that face the firm and the problems of risk and uncertainty. Also useful is Begg *et al.* (1991).

A useful text on business strategy is Johnson and Scholes (1990). Parker and Stacey (1994) provide a very useful and thought provoking analysis of chaos theory and its implications for management and economics.

CHAPTER 6

Forecasts for the OECD countries are provided biannually in the OECD *Economic Outlook*, and the London Business School *Economic Outlook* and the *National Institute Economic Review* (both quarterly) also provide commentary on the world economy.

Useful books on macroeconomic forecasting include Wallis *et al.* (1987) and Keating (1985). A wider treatment of business forecasting in general is given in Holden *et al.* (1990) and Whitley (1994).

CHAPTER 7

The excellent book by Brett (1991) explains in simple but comprehensive terms details of foreign-exchange markets and the institutions and businesses operating in them. A very good book on multinational finance is Buckley (1992) while Grimwade (1989) gives details of recent patterns of international trade, production and investment. Taylor (1995) provides an up-to-date summary of tests of exchange rate theories.

CHAPTER 8

Bain and Howells (1985) provide an introductory account of UK monetary policy, Dennis *et al.* (1982) give a detailed account of the institutional structure of the UK financial sector and Hall (1987) concentrates on financial innovation and deregulation. Llewellyn (1980) and Johnston (1983) focus on the international capital markets. A useful discussion of stock market efficiency and prediction is Mills (1992). Details of interest rate hedging can be found in Buckley (1992).

CHAPTER 9

A useful wide-ranging text is Hartley (1977), which discusses the case for and against intervention and various other aspects of policy. Grant and Shaw (1980) is also useful, as are Cross (1982) and Crystal (1983). See also Griffiths and Wall (1995) and Curwen (1990) for applied discussions in a UK context. More detail is provided by Healey (1993) and Crafts (1993). Good texts on regional issues are Armstrong H and Taylor J (1993) and Townroe P and Martin R (1992).

References

Armstrong, H. and Taylor, M. (1993) *Regional Economics and Policy*, London: Harvester Wheatsheaf.

Artis, M. (1984) *Macroeconomics*, Oxford: Oxford University Press.

Artis, M and Lewis, M.K. (1991) *Money in Britain*, Oxford: Philip Allan.

Bain, K. and Howells, R.G.A. (1985) *Monetary Economics*, London: Longman.

Beck, P. (1981) *Corporate Plans for an Uncertain Future*, London: Shell UK.

Begg, D., Fischer, S. and Dornbusch, R. (1991) *Economics*, 3rd edn, New York: McGraw-Hill.

Blake, D. (1993) *A Short Course of Economics*, Maidenhead: McGraw-Hill.

Bootle, R. (1996a) Interest fears are overdone. *Sunday Times*, 25 February.

Bootle, R. (1996b) *The Death of Inflation – Surviving and Thriving in the Zero Era*, London: Nicholas Braley.

Brett, M. (1991) *How to Read the Financial Pages*, 3rd edn, London: Hutchinson.

Buckley, A. (1992) *Multinational Finance*, 2nd edn, New York: Prentice Hall.

Central Statistical Office (1991a) *Economic Trends*, (449).

Central Statistical Office (1991b) *Economic Trends*, (457).

Central Statistical Office (1995) *Economic Trends*, (502).

Central Statistical Office (annual) *Financial Statistics*, London: HMSO.

Church, K., Mitchell, P., Smith, P. and Wallis, K. (1995) *National Institute Economic Review*, **3** (95), 59–72.

Coyle, D. (1966) Optimists and pessimists alike line up predictions for the year. *Independent*, 21 March.

Crafts, N.F.R. (1993) Can de-industrialisation seriously damage your wealth? *IEA, Hobart Paper*, **120**, London: IEA.

Cross, R. (1982) *Economic Theory and Policy in the United Kingdom*, Oxford: Martin Robertson.

Crystal, K.A. (1983) *Controversies in Macroeconomics*, 2nd edn, Oxford: Philip Allan.

Curwen, P. (1990) *Understanding the UK Economy*, London: Macmillan.

Davidson, J.E.H., Hendry, D.F., Srba, F. and Yeo, S. (1978) Econometric modelling of aggregate time series relationship between consumption and income in the United Kingdom, *Economic Journal*, **88**, 661–92.

Davies, G. (1996) Can we really cut spending to Asian levels? *Independent*, 26 February.

Davis, E.W. and Pointon, J. (1994) *Finance and the Firm: an Introduction to Corporate Finance*, Oxford: Oxford University Press.

Delors, J. (1989) *Report on Economic and Monetary Union in the European Community*, Luxemburg: Office for Official Publications of the European Communities.

Dennis, G.E.J., Hall, M., Llewellyn, D. and Nellis, G.J. (1982) *The Framework of United Kingdom Monetary Policy*, London: Heinemann.

Donne, M. and Friedman, A. (1982) The fight Sir Freddie lost. *Financial Times*, 6 February.

Dornbusch, R. and Fischer, S. (1990) *Macroeconomics*, 5th edn, New York: McGraw-Hill.

Easton, W.W. (1990) The interest rate transmission mechanism in the United Kingdom and overseas. *Bank of England Quarterly Bulletin*, **30**(2), May.

Eltis, W. (1995) *How Much of the UK Competitiveness Gap Has Been Closed?* London: The Foundation for Manufacturing and Industry.

Friedman, B. (1977) Financial flow variables and the short run determination of lend term interest rates. *Journal of Political Economy*, **85**(4), 661–89.

Gilmour, I. (1983) *Britain Can Work*, Oxford: Martin Robertson.

Goodhart, C.A.E., McMahon, P.C. and Ngama Y.L. (1992) Does the forward premium/discount help to predict the future change in the exchange rate? *Scottish Journal of Political Economy*, **39**(2), 129–40.

Grant, R.M. and Shaw, G.K. (1980) *Current Issues in Economic Policy*, Oxford: Philip Allan.

Griffiths, A. and Wall, S. (1995) *Applied Economics*, 6th edn, London: Longman.

Grimwade, N. (1989) *International Trade*, London: Routledge.

Hall, M. (1987) *Financial Deregulation*, London: Macmillan.

Hartley, K. (1977) *Problems of Economic Policy*, London: Allen and Urwin.

Healey, N.M. (1993) *Britain's Economic Miracle, Myth or Reality?* London: Routledge.

Hendry, D. F. (1983) Econometric modelling: the 'consumption function' in retrospect. *Scottish Journal of Political Economy*, **30**(3), 193–220.

HM Treasury (1990) *Comparison of Outside Forecasts*, London: HM Treasury.

HM Treasury (1995) *Forecasts for the UK Economy* (103).

HM Treasury (1996) *Comparison of Outside Forecasts*, London: HM Treasury.

Holden, K., Peel, D.A. and Thompson, J.L. (1990) *Economic Forecasting: an Introduction*, Cambridge: Cambridge University Press.

Johnson, G. and Scholes, K. (1990) *Exploring Corporate Strategy*, 2nd edn, London: Prentice Hall.

Johnston, R.B. (1983) *The Economics of the Euromarkets*, London: Macmillan.

Kay, J. (1993) *The Foundations of Corporate Success: How Business Strategies Add Value*, Oxford: Oxford University Press.

Keating, G. (1985) *The Production and Use of Forecasts*, London: Methuen.

Kettell, B. (1989) The 1987 stock market crash: are there any lessons for financial market theory? *Occasional Paper 4*, London: Department of Business Studies, City of London Polytechnic.

Keynes, J.M. (1936) *The General Theory of Employment, Interest and Money*, London: Macmillan.

Layard, R. (1986) *How to Beat Unemployment*, Oxford: Oxford University Press.

Llewellyn, D.T. (1980) *International Financial Integration*, London: Macmillan.

Lucas, R.E. (1976) Econometric policy evaluations: a critique, in K. Brunner and A.H. Meltzer (eds) *The Phillips Curve and Labour Markets*, Carnegie Rochester Conferences in Public Policy, vol. 1, Amsterdam: North Holland, pp. 19–46.

Lumby, S. (1984) *Investment Appraisal*, 2nd edn, Wokingham: Van Nostrand Reinhold.

Marsh, P. (1993) The art of guesswork. *Financial Times*, 30 April.

Meese, R.A. and Rogoff, K. (1983) Empirical exchange rate models of the seventies. Do they fit out of sample? *Journal of International Economics*, **14**, 3–24.

Mills, T.C. (1992) Predicting the unpredictable, science and guesswork in financial market forecasting. *IEA, Occasional Paper 87*, London: IEA.

Office of National Statistics (1996) *Economic Trends*, (518), December.

Office of National Statistics (1996/7) *Economic Trends*, Annual Supplement.

Organization for Economic Co-operation and Development (1991) *Historical Statistics*, Paris: OECD.

Organization for Economic Co-operation and Development (1996) *Economic Outlook*, Paris: OECD.

Osler, C.L. (1994) High foreign real interest rates and investment in the 1990s. *Federal Reserve Bank of New York, Quarterly Review*, Spring.

Parker, D. and Stacey, R. (1994) Chaos, management and economics. *IEA Hobart Paper*, **125**, London: IEA.

Parker, H. (1995) *Taxes, Benefits and Family Life*, London: IEA.

Peck, J. (1993) Tales of the unexpected: a polemic against employment forecasting. *Regional Studies*, **27**(1), 73–5.

Peters, T. (1987) *Thriving on Chaos: Handbook for a Management Revolution*, London: Macmillan.

Pilbeam, K. (1994) Chartists, fundamentalists and simpletons: an evaluation of alternative exchange rate trading strategies. *British Review of Economic Issues*, **16**(39) June, 65–83.

Plymouth Business School (1996), *Insight*, Plymouth: University of Plymouth.

Porter, M. (1990) *The Competitive Advantage of Nations*, London: Macmillan.

Pratten, C. (1986) The importance of giant companies. *Lloyds Bank Review*, **159**, January, 33–48.

Pratten, C. (1990) *Applied Macroeconomics*, 2nd edn, Oxford; Oxford University Press.

Rostow, W.W. (1978) *The World Economy, History and Prospect*, London: Macmillan.

Sunday Times (1996) Underhand competition. *Sunday Times*, 25 February.

Tanzi, V. and Schuknecht, L. (1995) The growth of government and the reform of the state in industrial countries. *IMF Working Paper*, December.

Taylor, M. (1995) Exchange rate modelling and macro fundamentals: failed partnership or open marriage. *British Review of Economic Issues*, **17**(42), June, 1–41.

Tobin, J. (1981) The monetarist counter-revolution today – an appraisal. *Economic Journal*, **91**(361), March, 3.

Townroe, P. and Martin, R. (1992) *Regional Development in the 1990s*, London: Jessica Kingsley.

Turner, P. (1989) Investment: theory and evidence. *Economic Review*, **6**(3).

Wallace, P. (1996) Mixed blessings in the two way flows of foreign investment. *Independent*, 22 February.

Wallis, K.F., Andrews, M.J., Bell, D.N.F., Fisher, P.G. and Whitley, J.D. (1987) *Models of the United Kingdom Economy: a Fourth Review*, Oxford: Oxford University Press.

Weiner, M.J. (1981) *English Culture and the Decline of the English Spirit*, Cambridge: Cambridge University Press.

Whitley, J. (1994) *A Course in Macroeconomic Modelling and Forecasting*, Brighton, Sussex: Harvester Wheatsheaf.

Index